WHERE the MAGIC HAPPENS

A JOURNEY TO INNER SPACE

DR. RHONDA K. RODGERS

EDITED BY CAROLYN MARSDEN
AND LESLIEE ANTONETTE, PH.D.

Abhinna LLC
PO Box 3298
Wrightwood, CA. 92397

ISBN PAPERBACK: 979-8-9985752-0-4
ISBN EBOOK: 979-8-9985752-1-1

Library of Congress Control Number: 2025937914

Cover design by Fixy

Interior design by Molly Mortimer, Mayfly book design, Minneapolis, MN
Printed in the USA

DEDICATION

This journey involved many teachers who entered my experience at the perfect time to nurture, challenge, and propel me into developing skills for mental, emotional, and spiritual well-being. This book is dedicated to these guides and ancestors. This book is also dedicated to all of those who still suffer and perhaps have no idea why or what to do to change the course of their lives.

CONTENTS

ABOUT THE AUTHOR

D r. Rhonda K. Rodgers is an unwavering pathfinder, continually testing her skills and endurance in exhilarating environments. From scaling the ancient stone ruins of Machu Picchu to navigating the harsh terrain as a co-pilot for the Mexican 1000 off-road rally, Dr. Rodgers revels in pushing the limits.

As a psychologist and researcher, she is equally intrigued with challenging the boundaries between science and self. Earning her MBA from Pepperdine University and a Ph.D. in Organizational Behavior from Claremont Graduate University, Dr. Rodgers seamlessly integrates her life experiences into her work.

Her innovative approach is deeply rooted in a desire to add a personal touch to the scientific landscape, help others gain deeper insights into themselves, and foster a better understanding of Inner Space—where the magic happens. To learn more about Dr. Rodgers' transformative journey and to discover your own, visit www.drrhondarodgers.com.

—Leandra Moreno-Prince

FOREWORD

Rhonda Rodgers has crafted a deeply personal and courageous narrative—an intimate account of one woman's journey inward. Rhonda is a seeker at her core: a soul yearning for peace, truth, and a life aligned with her deepest self. Her story is compelling, and a mirror is held up to the reader, a gentle invitation for self-reflection on the quiet questions many of us carry.

Rhonda shares moments of profound transformation throughout these pages—thresholds, where pain met awareness, and contemplative practice illuminated a new way forward. She describes one such moment with striking clarity: sitting in stillness, mind calm, body at rest, expecting nothing. And in that quiet, an answer emerged—simple and powerful: Just do today to the best of your ability. She interweaves contemplative practices that the reader can engage in to begin to practice the methods that aided in her journey.

That single instruction became a turning point, sparking a cascade of changes. She began rebuilding her life from the inside out. But before those outward shifts could take place, she had to confront the inner architecture of distraction—the mental diversions and emotional masks that had long kept her from her true self.

This book is both a map for the weary traveler and a mirror for the soul ready to awaken. Through practice and presence, it reveals how we can transform our innate wisdom into tangible actions—ones that heal, uplift, and reconnect us to our truest selves. Rhonda's reflections gently remind us that while the journey may be marked by suffering and self-doubt, it also opens space for peace, calm, and deep renewal. And that journey begins not outside of us, but within.

She courageously shares how trauma had held her in the grip of catastrophic thought cycles—relics of a long-ago pain still echoing through the present. She draws from the wisdom of many guides and the insight of her teacher, Geshe Dorji Damdul, who once said, "we are bullied by our minds." For years, that bully held her hostage. And yet, through her journey, she found a way to silence it. A quiet but profound liberation followed—a reclamation of agency, clarity, and self-compassion.

Rhonda offers her transparent and candid story as an inspiration—a spark to help ignite your own healing. She invites you to look beyond the façade you may have presented to the world, and instead, explore the vast inner landscape that patiently waits for your attention. She encourages you to work with your mind, to make it a peaceful home; to listen to your body, and let it guide you toward integration. She hopes you will begin choosing how your day unfolds, rather than being ruled by conditioned thought patterns and old narratives.

This book is a gift—an offering of truth, vulnerability, and hope. May it be a companion to you as you step into your own becoming.

—Elaine Miller-Karas, LCSW,
Executive Director Emeriti of the Trauma Resource Institute

INTRODUCTION

It was a magnificent spring day. The sun was just beginning to peek over the foothills of the San Gabriel Mountains, casting a light-purple hue across the silvery thread of highways leading from the Inland Empire to the city of Los Angeles. I climbed upon my dream ride, a beautiful BMW 1200 GS motorcycle and idled the engine, noting the exquisite smell of oil warming in the crankcase. I tapped my toe and the bike clunked into first gear. The chill of the morning air evaporated as the windscreen deflected the frosty breeze over the top of my helmet and away from the warmth emanating from the heated hand grips.

This morning commute had once been my favorite time of day, when I was in a happier place. Once upon a time I found great joy in the simplest of things like riding a motorcycle, or savoring the taste of morning coffee, but those joyful experiences had been slowly dying, day by day, and month by month. Until I found myself stuck in a robotic process of waking, dressing, driving to work, driving home, and then doing it all again. And today was the culmination of this darkness. As I darted in and out of traffic, a single question circled through my mind, *would it be so bad if I died today*? My life had become complicated. My marriage was a disaster, my career was ending, and I had no idea what to do next.

I became convinced that no matter which option I chose, I would make the wrong move and end up worse off than my current place of hopelessness. This whirlwind of anxiety had been escalating for weeks until the inevitable happened—mental, physical, and emotional breakdown.

I entered my place of work but could no longer pull myself together and face the day. I was in survival mode and needed a place to escape the demons in my own mind. I lowered my head, tears streaming down my face, avoiding eye contact with coworkers and made my way to a bathroom stall. I was desperately seeking clarity but encountered a tornado of tragic thoughts and indescribable confusion. I knew that I needed to change something, but was paralyzed by the idea of change, and had no idea where to begin. Every mental scenario that I ran created greater fear and anxiety. And it was at this moment that I realized I was out of options.

As I sat balled up on the toilet seat, with my head in my hands and my eyes tightly shut, I stopped running scenarios in my mind and instead asked for help. Who I asked I cannot tell you, it may have been God, or some dearly departed ancestor, or perhaps even a benevolent order of the cosmos. But at this very moment an amazing warmth descended from my scalp and traveled slowly down to my abdomen. Every muscle in my body relaxed. A deep burst of air penetrated the depths of my lungs and a feeling that everything was going to be okay washed over me. The three-foot by five-foot industrial metal partition expanded into infinite space. At that moment I was transported from a place of hopelessness to awe.

The question was no longer what can I do, but what can't I do? I had entered the field of infinite possibility! I began to breathe again and intuited that if I could find my way through one more day that more information would come to light. This glimpse of hope was enough to carry me forward. Some might call this a spiritual experience, and others might call it hitting bottom. In my story it was both. More importantly, the experience catalyzed a desire to utilize this power to recreate my life. There were answers out there that were not of my own mental creation. This was an exciting proposition.

You may be asking why I didn't notice my life slowly deteriorating. How had I failed to realize that my inner world had become a never-ending barrage of distressing thoughts, images, and sensations? How had I ignored the constant pounding heart, shallow breath, and dry mouth? The truth is that it was a slow, insidious journey. I can't remember when the feelings began, but for as long as I can remember, I would awaken with *sensations*, feelings of danger in my body, which triggered thoughts of past events, and tactical plans to avoid these scenarios. Why does the body and mind react in such a way? Quite simply, this is a physiological survival strategy that occurs without conscious awareness.

The word that I chose to define this period of life was *chaos*, which describes a system that is extremely sensitive to change. In technical terms, I was experiencing the effects of *allostatic load*. Wear and tear on the body resulting from chronic or repeated stress. After years of constant fear and worry from my life circumstances, long work hours, job insecurity, and strained relationships, my body began to physiologically change from repeated activation of this biological stress response. Over time the rational planning network in my brain was less available for problem solving, and, as the years wore on, I became more frazzled and more exhausted mentally, emotionally, and physically.

These prolonged levels of stress led to feelings of anxiety and depression, and contributed to my reliance upon alcohol, which further impacted my health and relationships. I believed that I could pull myself together through sheer willpower but failed to notice the progressively poor life choices that I was making. I was in a downward spiral and had zero tools to get myself back on track. Sometimes this is exactly the scenario that we need to seek out new information. The important point is that although I fell down, I got back up and continued to explore and discover new ways of living. If you follow the suggestions in this book, you too can find a way to get back up and begin your own journey to well-being.

HOW TO USE THIS BOOK

The information presented here does not follow the biomedical model of solely relying upon someone or something else to address our mental health and subsequent well-being. Instead, over the past decade I have experimented with many methods of self-directed healing, which are distilled and offered here as a conceptual framework I have written about in academic journals, Mental and Emotional Self-Management (MESM). My goal in sharing this information is to communicate a practical set of tools which can be mastered through application and practice, in the day-to-day laboratory of your life.

In certain wisdom traditions of the world, the act of using one's own life experiences to overcome obstacles is known as the warrior's path (Trungpa, 2007). This is what we must do, we must become warriors. We use life challenges as opportunities to turn inward, come to know our own bodies and minds, and then train to heal those parts of us that are not in alignment with our highest self, or our full potential as human beings.

Before we get into the practical business of healing, let's speak briefly about the metaphysical. I wish to share a few words about the topic of *God* and will defer to Alan W. Watts, a philosopher, scholar, and practitioner of human *being*, who in my estimation put it best: "In this universe there is one great energy, and we have no name for it" (Watts, 2019). Whenever I refer to God, Universal Spirit, Brahma, or any other written description of this *great energy*, I invite you to interpret this concept as you feel most comfortable. Please substitute whichever idea or word that is most appropriate for your own experience. As you will soon learn, I have no aspiration to explore the ineffable and am more interested in communicating my experiences without creating a barrier between us. I also ask that you keep an open mind toward your own definition of this great energy.

The path to healing is not a linear journey, there will be periods of progress and periods of challenge. But you are exactly where you need to be to do the work at hand. And yes, this process can get uncomfortable, as we become aware of sensations, such as tingling, knots, and other felt senses of experiences in the body, along with the accompanying emotions that have long been ignored. As we bring these experiences into our awareness, we discover that we have a choice. We can continue to ignore, or we can acknowledge the information, experience the sensations, then release the energy, and move forward. Awareness is the first step to healing, and despite the challenges, this path of personal growth is worth the time and effort.

The chapters in this book are organized into three sections: Exploration, Discovery, and Practice. As you move through the material, I invite you to utilize these same portals to facilitate your own journey. In Exploration, we become willing to explore our own life circumstances and to assess where we might need growth. In Discovery, through exploration we discover certain changes we may need to undertake in order to experience the growth that we desire. The final step is to Practice. We learn to use tools for transformation in our daily lives through developing a routine to use them. Exercise boxes are nested throughout each phase of the book to help facilitate your own personal journey. Practice pauses are scattered throughout the text, to provide opportunities to integrate skills for mental and emotional self-management into your daily routine.

I am happy that you are here and invite you to awaken the warrior within. This journey will change your life if you are willing and persistent. Without a willingness to do things differently, we remain stuck in outdated attitudes and behaviors. Without persistence, we will not see results. But fear not, this is a journey and no matter what detours may happen along the way, you can always recalibrate and return to the warrior's path. It is who you are and your birthright as a human being. Are you ready to reclaim your power?

EXPLORATION

The Climb to Kearsarge Pass. Photo Credit: J. Bruno

CHAPTER 1

WHERE AM I?

I needed to get out of town and out of my own head. A friend reached out asking for a favor, which presented the perfect opportunity to do just that. Justin and I met at the Onion Valley Campground of the Sierra Nevada in California, at 5am. Our objective was to climb Kearsarge Pass (11,760 ft) and then descend to the Charlotte Lake Campground to resupply a group of friends who were hiking the John Muir Trail.

Maybe sleeping three hours and then driving to the trailhead in the middle of the night wasn't such a great idea. But here we were, and friends were waiting, so no time for second guesses. The first three miles up the trail were tough, I focused on placing one boot in front of the other as we slowly gained altitude. I would occasionally turn back to view the valley below and marvel at the spectacular views from the rapidly ascending trail. As we climbed, the scent of the parched desert trail was replaced with the sweet and pungent aroma of pine trees. We rounded the corner to Big Pothole Lake that was still covered in ice and I suddenly remembered why I did this oftentimes grueling thing that we call backpacking. The air was crisp. There was no cell phone reception. No distractions other than the occasional urge for a bite of protein bar and swig of water. My mind was as clear as the mountain air and suddenly a joy returned to my heart reminiscent of the carefree excitement of the last day of school before summer vacation. I was giddy for no reason other than I was completely in the moment, on a mountain, with nothing to do but hike the mountain.

Kearsarge Pass, Inyo National Forest, CA. Photo Credit: J. Bruno

We reached the pass and dropped our packs to marvel at the desert valley to our backs and the lush basin of lakes that lay before us. A gentleman to my left commented that it was a gift to be on the mountain that day. And it was. He went on to say that it was his birthday, and that hiking was the reason he had made it to 86 years of age. We all congratulated him although none of us were surprised. This gentleman in his 86th year of life had crystal blue eyes and a weathered face that spoke of no regrets. He too was in the moment, sharing this space of childlike awe, as we all sat enraptured by the sights and sounds of the eastern Sierra.

I am a seeker in search of moments of clarity; vigilant for clues as to how to make these moments last. That is why I am writing this book. I am on a journey away from stress, distractions, and looking for relief in all the wrong places. This place I seek to explore is the Inner world. A place that many humans, including myself, have chosen not to investigate for fear of what we might discover. We have good reason. We have been taught not to tamper with the domain of doctors, psychiatrists, and clergy. But answer this honestly, who knows more about you than

YOU? The unknown will remain hidden until we muster the courage to undertake this remarkable journey to Inner Space!

My hope is that this book will be a resource for you in your own exploration. I ask that you give yourself permission to move through this journey in any way that resonates with you. The mind, body, and spirit are each complex phenomena and whatever pace at which you interact with this book and your unique experiences will be good enough. Also, understand that we cannot explore the inner workings of our experiences in a linear fashion or expect to figure it all out by the second chapter. This work takes time and patience.

In the pages that follow, I will honestly share with you my personal experiences, the healing that is possible, and how life can evolve into a happier, less stressful existence, moment by moment, and day by day. No matter what your current circumstances, I ask that you be patient with yourself and stay the course, for this is a remarkable journey and each of us must forge our own unique path to well-being.

Very Tired but Still Smiling. Somewhere on the High Sierra Trail, King's Canyon National Park, CA. Photo Credit: unknown.

CHAPTER 2

HOW DID I GET HERE?

All knowledge of reality starts from experience and ends in it.

—*Albert Einstein*

I am a biopsychologist, which is a fancy term for someone who seeks to understand human behavior through biology. Better stated, I study how our mind interprets signals from our own bodies and then combines this information with signals from the outside environment to create what we call reality. As such, I am both a researcher and a social experiment, meaning that I seek to understand why I behave in ways that completely defy intelligence and logic. Central to this task is an exploration of that which I understand to be me: the body, the mind, and the *spirit*, or our highest potential. You may not have connected the dots that you are here for a purpose. Imagine this purpose is within you right now waiting to be discovered. As we begin to align these elements of being, your purpose will come into focus.

The consistent persona that I recognize and identify as "me," from early childhood is a researcher in love with observation and experimentation. I love to try new things, observe what is working, what isn't, and then try again and again to make things better. And this, my friends, is why I wrote this book. I am an expert at this trial-and-error process, and like all researchers, I love to share what I have found that works, as well as, what did not work so well. Let us begin with the latter.

I grew up in the United States and was taught from childhood that all you need in life is a good job. If you have a good job, then everything else will fall into place. I followed this advice and had my first job at 14 restocking the shelves of the local convenience store. It was walking distance from my parent's house and paid enough to supply what I needed in life, snacks, and quarters for foosball and air hockey. My parents were not around much and when they were, it was not pleasant. There was lots of screaming, crying, and throwing of objects. My parents had followed the same formula, get a good job and everything else will fall into place. I knew at an early age that this logic was incorrect but had no resources at this point in life to formulate a better plan.

My childhood was spent in the South where one goes to religion for answers to life's problems. School friends would regularly approach to ask if I had accepted Jesus Christ as my personal savior. It seemed this might be the answer to the screaming, shouting, and sleepless nights, so I went with a friend to the local church. I joined a club that awarded points for memorizing Bible verses. I excelled at learning and soon had several badges and little plastic reminders of Jesus' sacrifices for me, a plastic Jesus on the cross, and a plastic replica of a Bible open to the 10 Commandments. But the uneasiness of my life did not stop. I read the Bible and learned stories of love, vengeance, punishment, and fear—constant fear. I understood fear. I was already in fear. I lived a life of constant vigilance; each day when I awoke the fear began, fear of leaving my room to face the day, fear of coming home from school to another family explosion, fear of not fitting in at school, fear of not fitting in at church, and fear of not finding someone who could help me.

It soon became apparent that my friend who invited me to church was content with the little plastic rewards. I began to notice that her parents never talked to one another. We would all ride together in the family station wagon to church, in silence, except when we would pass a strip club or dive bar. Then, my friend and her little brother would sing in unison "burn down, burn down." I was puzzled; why would Christians wish for arson, loss of property, and perhaps loss of life? There were other things going on that troubled me about this new church. The preacher's son was a notorious bully. All of the parents and the preacher were aware of this, but no one seemed to care. I asked one of the adults in my Bible study why no one stopped him. "Boys will be boys," she replied. Then one day the mother of my church friend collapsed in the hallway outside of my Bible study classroom. She was a heavyset woman, and I stood back expecting her husband to rush to her aid. Instead, he looked at her in disgust and walked away. My heart sank, and I knew that this was not the place, nor the people that I could turn to for guidance out of my own suffering.

The day after this event was the day that I had been told to come forward at the end of service to accept Jesus as my personal savior. I would get a special embroidered patch for this action, which I could then wear proudly on my jacket as a proclamation of my membership as a Christian. I was told what a special day this would be and how my life would change forever. The sermon began; I listened carefully to the words and heard, again, messages of fear, vengeance, and punishment that were the constant refrain on Sundays. I was told that this was a special day that would change my life, and to expect miraculous feelings of Jesus' love. But I felt nothing but fear and confusion. I stopped listening to the sermon and knew from that moment that I would not walk forward at the end of the service. The time came, and the preacher invited all of those who were ready to accept Jesus Christ as their Lord and personal savior to walk forward. My club looked at me anxiously. My friend, her mother and father all motioned for me to get going. I sat there, confident that what I needed was not going to appear if I performed this ritual and more importantly that I would be lying to God if I walked forward. The service ended. The boys and girls who were saved received their patches, and the ride home was especially quiet.

The mother and father of my friend were disgusted with me as demonstrated by their occasional glances back at me in the rear-view mirror. The chorus of "burn down, burn down" occasionally broke the silence of the trip. The family never returned to pick me up. My church friend still talked to me at school but made it clear that we were no longer "friends." I returned to my tumultuous life, relieved that I was no longer in the company of this church family. It took me many years to understand the difference between love and punishment and even longer to understand that the two cannot coexist in a healthy relationship, whether it be with another human being or with a power greater than oneself. But it took me only one moment to understand that God, as I understand this Spirit of the Universe, accepts me just as I am, and will never withhold love from me or anyone else. From this moment forward, I understood that religion is a man-made construction, while spirituality is something greater than any human can conceive of or explain, and from that moment forward in my young life, I chose spirituality.

I was an avid reader at this age and fortunate to have access to a range of books. The Science Fiction of Ray Bradbury, the poetry of Dorothy Parker, and stories upon stories of adventure and overcoming great obstacles all helped me to escape to another life, another planet, an alternate reality. A friend introduced me to marijuana around this same time, at age 13. I did not care for the acrid smell, the taste on my tongue, or the burning feeling of smoke hitting the back of my throat, but it was nice to feel comfortable, if only for an hour or two. This became my drug of choice, a temporary fix to a deeper problem.

One day, something wonderful occurred. I was walking through the rows of the school library, searching for my next escape and I found the book that would change my life. I read a few pages right there in between the stacks of books and felt calmness, stillness, and hope. A lightness filled my heart. What had just happened!?

I sat down on the well-worn carpet and read further. The answer to my quandary of how to get out of this misery was in MY power. I just had to create the space to do it on my own. That book was *Siddhartha*, by Herman Hesse, a story about a seeker of peace and meaning in life, as well as instruction on how to find inner peace in a tumultuous world, and my world was just that.

My mother was diagnosed with Bipolar Affective Disorder (BPAD) when I was in elementary school and her mood swings were fast and furious. At the time I had no idea how terrifying this disease was for my mother. Mania can come with intense symptoms such as hallucinations and loss of physical control, while the depressive state can steal any ability to feel joy or pleasure with life. As an adult, I have been able to develop a sense of compassion for the extremes of thought and sensation experienced by those with BPAD and have a profound sense of empathy for anyone suffering from this devastating disease, however as a child, I was terrified by my mother's behavior.

PRACTICE PAUSE: BELLY BREATHING

You can practice belly breathing anytime that you need to bring your nervous system back into balance and restore calm to the body and mind.

Place one hand on your heart, as a gesture of self-soothing, and the other hand on your belly.

Let the belly rise as you inhale and fall as you exhale.

Do not force the movements of the belly but rather let the natural motion of your torso expand on the in-breath and contract on the out-breath.

Breathe slowly and patiently for 5 belly breaths.

Notice the sensations in the body that arise after 5-10 belly breaths.

If you like what you are feeling keep going!

When the manic side hit, my mother would lash out at everyone in the house. I could at least escape to my room, but my stepfather remained, taking her verbal and physical abuse full force. It was during one such rage that I found my first mantra, taken from the pages of *Siddhartha*: "I can think, I can wait, I can fast", which to me meant that I didn't have to be swept away by the hurricane of emotional and physical turmoil in the next room. By slowing my mind and connecting to a calmness within, I experienced a peacefulness that I had not known before. As I came to discover, the central character of the book, Siddhartha was also a researcher who, just like me, wanted to find some peace and serenity in a chaotic world.

But the chaos continued, I grew older, and the tension between my mother and I grew stronger. By the age of 15, I was tall enough to fight back- to yell back, block her punches- put up a fight. This unleashed the beast. She became dangerous and her behavior changed from throwing things around the house, to throwing things at me. A pint jar of mayonnaise missed my head by half an inch and exploded against the wall. I avoided brain injury that day and my mother avoided prison. I retreated to my room and the mantra came to mind: "I can think, I can wait, I can fast." I was calm, still, and no longer in fear. In this moment of peace, I found clarity and direction. I intuitively knew that if I kept a cool head, I could curtail my mother's rage against me. Up until this moment I had been at the mercy of my environment. But miraculously a way forward appeared, and I came up with a plan. At the age of eighteen I would be a legal adult and could leave my parent's house. But I could not take three more years of this terror. I had to find a quicker escape and moving away to attend college was the answer. I could leave home upon graduation from high school, at age 17, and save my sanity.

I moved out of my parent's house and found a barback job that allowed me to work part time and make enough money to live off of while in school. The world I entered at The Lighthouse was pure fantasy. Everyone seemed happy, no yelling or screaming, no throwing of objects, just booze, drugs, and parties every night. I would come in a few hours early to sit in this wonderland of stale cigarette smoke and sour speed racks, for a pre-shift gin and tonic. I worked an 8-hour shift punctuated with customers buying me the occasional shot of tequila for my service and would end each evening with a post-shift margarita, the "Santos", a wonderful 100 proof concoction created by the head bartender. My drug of choice had shifted from weed to alcohol. I spent 10 hours, four days a week, in the proverbial candy factory.

One evening my bar manager introduced me to his best friend's wife, who was visiting from Miami. I served her drinks, and we chatted until the bar closed. She and her husband were making plans to sail around the world for a year. He was back home in Miami readying the boat, and she was only in town for the night, on her way to join him with the preparations. What an amazing life she had! Excitement, love, adventure, she had a plan for living. I was enthralled with her existence and wanted to be just like her.

I closed the bar and walked around to the back apartment where the bar manager lived to drop the cash and books from the evening close. I stopped short and found my new friend dancing naked in the window as the bar manager, her husband's "best friend", smiled approvingly from the couch. I put the cash box next to the apartment door and walked away. This was not the life I wanted: booze, lies, adultery, fantasy, and escape. I was exhausted from escaping life. I wanted to embrace life, to feel at peace, and to create a new reality that I felt was possible in my heart. Life went on like this for months, my drinking escalated, my college grades tanked, and it soon became apparent that this was not working. I had no idea what to do next.

What was I searching for? A new place to live, a new city, a new job, a new relationship? The Galveston Seawall, a magnificent, ten-foot high, concrete structure designed to thwart the deluge of hurricane tides, seemed like the place to go. I walked up and down the Seawall, running different scenarios in my head. My mind was spinning, and I needed to calm down so I could figure this thing out. But I had no idea how to calm down without a drink or drug. I paused for a moment and the words of *Siddhartha* re-entered my awareness, "I can think, I can wait, I can fast." I sat cross legged and gazed across The Gulf of Mexico. I took a deep breath and asked for guidance. I sat quietly, mind calm, body still, expecting nothing. Within moments an answer came, "just do today to the best of your ability." A list of steps then became clear for a course correction. I would move back home, find a job unrelated to alcohol, go back to school at a community college, save money, and then get my own place. Through calming the chatter in my mind, using a process I called meditation, I created space to receive inspiration, through a practice I now call *connection*. I was able to find the clarity and motivation to move my life in a new direction. This experience was beyond serenity; it was communion with something much larger than me. A spiritual presence that was calming, loving, and all knowing.

It would be wonderful if I could tell you that I continued to meditate and connect from that day forward. But as time went on, the amazing experience that I had on the Seawall, slowing my mind to the point where I could connect with the calmness within, faded from memory and I returned to my only solution to the uncertainty of life, hard work.

I took classes at the local community college and put my full attention into studying. I found a good job unloading tractor trailers on the twilight shift. The 4 a.m. start time was a perfect scenario that allowed me to work part time to save money and still take a full load of college classes. I shifted my attention into my new job and was promoted to supervisor within six months. More money meant a new truck and moving into my own apartment. Life was good per the formula: good job and everything else falls into place. But things did not fall into place as promised. I was an angry person with a short temper. I was on edge, slept very little, and trusted no one.

My first serious romantic relationship in high school was with a female. I naively assumed that my parents and fellow students would be supportive of my authentic self, but the opposite occurred. I was encouraged to call it off, start dating a nice boy, and ask God for forgiveness. Keep in mind that at this point in history few gay people were represented in the media or society, and neither acceptance nor tolerance were on the table in my hometown. The options were to stay in the closet or risk physical harm. I chose to be who I was and hope for the best. Was it stressful? Hell yes! But I was unwilling to live a lie.

The hostility surrounding me was palpable. I was resented and felt resentment toward everyone. I was rising through the ranks of management and began a romantic relationship with a female co-worker that repeated everything I had learned as a child: isolation, detachment, suspicion, and distance. Lesbianism was not looked upon very favorably in this organization, or anywhere else in Texas, and the stress of being in a same sex relationship added another dimension of anxiety to my repertoire of feelings of uneasiness with the world. But things were shifting, I was supporting myself financially and the promise of an independent life created space in my head and heart to accept all of me, especially the angry, fearful and suspicious parts.

I awoke each morning with the same fear in the pit of my stomach that I had felt for the past 19 years. I was waiting for the volatility that was so common in childhood, and now that my mother was not in the next room, I had to create my own chaos. I did so by staying extremely busy and worrying about everything that was out of my control.

I worked harder and got another promotion. I quickly learned that if I put my personal life and well-being second to my work life, the promotions kept coming, as did the responsibility. And the money. I continued the chase and moved from Texas to New York, to New Jersey, and then to California. The jobs got bigger and according to the formula, so did the house, cars, and leisure activities, but not the happy family. I had grown up in an alcoholic/mental illness plagued household, as did both of my parents. I had no social model for any other behavior, so this is what I repeated in my own relationships. I took my first management job at the age of nineteen and twenty-five years later concluded that the formula was not working. I had moved through multiple careers, each of which fulfilled the requisite "good job" designation, but happiness was illusive.

The relationship with my female coworker lasted 20 years sheerly on codependence. I knew very little about the lovely human being that was my partner, and she knew even less about me, which over time led to a parting of lives. I cannot blame her for wanting out. Who wants to be married to a mentally, emotionally, and physically absent spouse? The trust and respect between us ended and this chapter of life came to a close.

I created two piles of personal belongings: necessary and unnecessary, and loaded all the unnecessary belongings into black plastic contractor bags, which I deposited at the local "Out of The Closet" second-hand store in Echo Park, California. It was amazing to see how much stuff I had accumulated that was of no practical use. There were multiple pairs of running shoes, only one of which was regularly worn, and 10 bottles of different fragrances, only two of which were less than full. How had I become so blind to my consumption of material crap?

I needed to get away from the routine of my old life. I took a leave of absence from my job and moved into a 10-foot by 8-foot room in a shared house in the Russian Village in Claremont, California. My belongings consisted of a few books, three changes of clothing, a bicycle, and a coffee maker. To the casual observer, it might seem that I was moving deeper into despair. But the freedom from all the stuff I *thought* I needed was immediate. In the center of this cyclone of change was an eye of calmness. Life was simplified. My choices were simplified.

For the first time in decades, I could put energy into me. So, I set about the painful and unpredictable work of healing. My days were broken into chunks of rest, exercise, and an occasional meal. I was sleeping 3-4 hours per night, punctuated by night terrors. I would awaken after leaping out of bed, in a cold sweat, heart pounding through my chest, wondering what the hell had just happened!

I lost 23 pounds and felt profound sadness for the loss of so many familiar things that were no longer in my life: the partner, dogs, friends, house in the hills, and the seeming certainty of these material things. Now that I had changed everything in my external world, it was time to make real and lasting changes in my internal world.

It occurred to me that I had not a single moment of peace in any 24-hour period that I could recollect. My mind raced endlessly both day and night. This led to the conclusion that I first needed a method to slow down the barrage of thoughts. Somewhere in my psyche the word *meditation* reappeared. I did an Internet search for meditation and the first technique that popped up was breath counting. I began the excruciating task of sitting in a chair and focusing on my breath. The Internet suggested that a session should be fifteen minutes in length, but for me this was unbearable. My thoughts were so uncomfortable that I felt as if I were drowning in them. I decided to do whatever length of breath counting I could manage. I sat and focused on my breath for 10 seconds and in those 10 seconds I felt a little better. This led to the conclusion, why not try for 20 seconds? I would sit for 20 seconds and feel even a little better. By the end of the first week of practice I could sit for a minute or two in peace, which abruptly ended when the tsunami of thoughts came crashing back, overpowering my fledgling meditation practice.

I not only needed a method to diminish my thoughts, but to dampen the overwhelming torrents of emotion that I experienced during meditation. A logical person could see that I was in no physical danger and that in reality I was sitting comfortably in my room. But, in my experience emotions are more powerful than any amount of logic. I began to wonder why these feelings appeared so real to me. Meditation offered a method to explore these intense feelings as an observer and to question reality.

Why would I experience fear with no immediate danger in my environment? Clearly this experience was being manufactured in my mind. With this awareness, it became easier to watch the thoughts come and go. My physical body was not yet on board with this new "observer"

EXERCISE: BREATH–COUNTING

Now would be a great time to learn the simple yet profound technique of breath counting. We are going to use the same practice as we did in belly breathing, but we are going to add the dimension of counting to give our mind something to do. I invite you to take a moment to notice how you feel both before and then after this practice.

Our breath is a powerful tool that can restore balance to the nervous system. Diaphragmatic or *belly breathing* uses the diaphragm of the body rather than the chest muscles, to engage a relaxation response in the nervous system.

Place one hand over your heart and one hand on the belly.

Breathe in and allow the belly or stomach area of your body to rise.

Breathe out and allow the belly to fall.

Take a slow, deep breath in, watch the belly rise, and slowly exhale, watching the belly fall. Count "1."

Take another slow refreshing in-breath, and at the end of the out-breath count "2".

With each breath try to breathe a bit deeper and a little slower.

Practice making the out-breath a little longer than the in-breath.

Continue practicing until you reach the count of 10 belly breaths.

Feel free to continue past the count of 10 if you need more relaxation.

Don't think about the future or worry about the past. Just focus on the rising and falling of the belly, and sensations of the breath as it enters and exits the body. This is a great antidote to a worried, distracted, or overwhelmed mind.

practice. As I watched the internal working of the emotions arising in the body, I noticed that the mind would add a storyline to every experience. It was as if one was feeding the other with material. As an observer of this body + mind experience or, for simplicity, the *bodymind*, I noticed and then resisted the experience whenever intense sensations of discomfort would arise. So intense, in fact, that during some instances I felt threatened enough to jump up to my feet and leave the apartment.

By the second week of observation practice, I could make it to 10 minutes before I had to dart out of my seat and find something else to do. As with breath counting, I felt that if I could make it through 10 minutes just watching and not getting wrapped up in the process, then 20 minutes would be possible somewhere in the future.

Now for some good news. There is no special training required to become an observer of the bodymind. You just need to understand the value of this practice. The nervous system is much like a software program coded through everyday experiences. Here's an example for you. I recently visited my parents and told them that my next stop would be my brother's house on the Gulf Coast. My mother ran upstairs and grabbed a roll of quarters for the toll road. I thanked her and headed south only to find that the coin toll booths had been replaced with cashless radar payment. My mother's database had not been updated with current reality. How often might this happen in your own experience? As an observer we begin to question everything.

The only requirement to get into observer mode is to watch the thoughts that arise in your own mind. At first it will be very enticing to jump into the waves of thoughts and storylines that our minds create and get swept away, but this takes us out of observer mode and back into the relentless torrent of the mind. With practice, this process of the bodymind creating endless loops of storylines and felt experiences of these storylines in the body, becomes more obvious. Therefore, practice is crucial to progress. Remember, there is no sleight of hand, no trickery, nothing out of the ordinary, and nothing to accomplish, other than to watch your thoughts and begin to notice how the mind and body work together to create a story that we assume is reality.

Occasionally folks will approach me to address a conflict they perceive between meditation and their chosen religion. If you fall into this

PRACTICE PAUSE: SPACE EXPLORATION

Find a quiet space away from distractions.

Set a timer for five minutes and take the first minute or two for breath counting. For the remainder of this session, I invite you to explore the space between your thoughts.

Simply notice where one thought ends and then rest in the space that exists before the next thought begins.

Try not to judge your ability because you are just getting started.

Become curious about what is going on in your inner world, at this very moment.

If this feels uncomfortable, then you are doing it right! The mind operates via old patterns and behaviors and new experiences create discomfort.

Just notice what comes up without trying to fix anything. You are now the observer of your thoughts and anything else that comes into awareness.

camp, then I ask you to define meditation as a prescription for mental health rather than a religious practice. For, as I have just explained, meditation is the gateway to becoming an observer of your internal experience. There are multiple methods of meditation, as well as different scientific and wisdom traditions that emphasize different types of meditation. I like to use physical exercise as an analogy that, like meditation, can be used to increase well-being. One can engage in cardio activities, strength training, stretching, or any combination of the above. Each type of activity is designed to influence a particular change within the physiology of the human body, so it goes with meditation. For the purpose of this book, let's focus on what can be accomplished through using meditation as a researcher, in search of a better understanding of our own inner worlds.

Through the practice of meditation and observation, greater awareness continued to develop and by the third week, I could safely watch thoughts and sensations coming and going for 15 minutes, without running for the door. You may find similar progress in your own meditation practice, or you may find that it takes much less time and effort to reach 15 minutes of meditation. Either way, if you are practicing daily, then you are doing it right.

It was about this time that I discovered two narratives taking place in my head. One telling me that this move to a new town was a fresh start and that I could create my life anew. The other was one of failure and pain. Who would leave a good job, nice house, and somewhat damaged marriage to the only person who would ever love me? Introspection was the process that helped me to not only discover the thoughts that were constantly rattling my psyche, but to also discern that they were not very helpful thoughts!

As I objectively watched my thoughts, without letting them run away with me, attaching myself to them or judging them, I realized that it was time for a new story of who *I* was. This newfound peace of mind also created space to believe that I had the power to change my life. A daily meditation practice was the first step in creating this new story.

Through meditation and introspection, I became aware that there was also a lot of good in my life, which for me was a huge shift in thinking. I had a loving stepfather who treated me as his own child, a grandmother who went to the ends of the earth to ensure that I felt loved and cared for, and a mother who, despite her mental illness, encouraged me to be everything that I could possibly dream of. My mother intuited that I would one day become a writer and over the years introduced me to various works of poetry, books on the creative process, and novels by her favorite authors. I was also blessed with a stream of love from friends and significant others who saw in me what I could not yet fathom, that I was a precious human being with innate goodness. This was the foundation that enabled me to believe that a better life was out there, waiting to be discovered. But what was I seeking? Why do so many of us have the suspicion that we are here to do something remarkable with this lifetime, but have no idea where to begin?

As with us all, my upbringing informed my worldview. The reality created through childhood experiences, informed my way of behaving as a young adult, which I chose not to question for many decades. It never occurred to me that I was living a story created by others. But slowly I came to realize that the old story kept me in the same experience of life, year after year, job after job, relationship after relationship. The names and locations changed, but the external world continued to mirror my internal state of body and mind. Chaos.

I knew that something was missing but could not put my finger on the exact problem. The words I would now use to describe this longing are *spiritual hunger*; a state of craving that cannot be fulfilled by material possessions or another human being. This realization began to taunt me. I would look to the outside world for clues as to who I was, or more accurately which identity to assume. Each time that I tried to fit into someone else's identity, it never worked out. I could not yet comprehend that the person I was looking for was already there, waiting for a spiritual connection. This being was a complex mix of fear and love, victim and warrior.

My mind had created a complex system of diversions to keep me from getting in touch with this inner soul. For years I had given in to these distractions to avoid discovering who I really was. I was now ready to explore the inside of me rather than the outer façade that I hid behind. The great thing about pain is that it is a wonderful catalyst for change. Once I had experienced enough psychic, emotional, and spiritual pain, I was willing to change the course of my life. Now I just needed a direction.

Sturtevant Trail. Angeles National Forest, CA. Photo Credit:
R.K. Rodgers

CHAPTER 3

FOLLOW THE SIGNS

T he house and backyard were filled to capacity with what I describe as Chris fans. Music and the scent of multiple potluck dishes wafted across the Claremont neighborhood from the impromptu gathering of locals who had come to pay tribute to Chris in the best way they knew how- a bluegrass sit in. Although Chris had left his physical body, his spiritual presence at this shindig was undeniable.

Chris was a river rapids guide, who smiled frequently, hugged deeply, rode his bike in flip flops, and played a mean guitar. As I sat there, hoping for a glimpse of Chris out of the corner of my eye, I recalled a gem of a message that he had shared with me some months earlier "focus on your path, not the obstacles." This advice was so simple, yet much deeper than I anticipated. In my eyes, Chris was the embodiment of the good life. After the initial ah-ha! this is important, I tucked this information away and waited to see when it might come in handy.

Just like you, I am on a quest for health, happiness, and a full life. Occasionally I get a precious clue, but what do I do with this information once it enters my awareness? If we are distracted either by inner chatter in the mind or external overstimulation of our modern world, it simply fades away. But if we are attentive, meaning that we can focus on where to insert this lesson, then we might notice how this information applies to us. Even if we have paid attention to these valuable clues, we can fall short in bringing them into practice. As you will learn throughout this book, we can begin to transform innate wisdom into positive behaviors, which have the potential to transform our lives.

I recalled a similar message to Chris' life instruction during my motorcycle training course: focus on where you want to go rather than what you are trying to avoid. This makes perfect sense if we want to avoid a hazard on the road, but what about a hazard in life, like staying in a dead-end job, or hanging onto a failing relationship? We may intuitively know that it's time to make a change, but once we throw human emotions into the mix, all bets are off.

WHY IS IT SO HARD TO CHANGE? MEET YOUR NERVOUS SYSTEM!

The journey from focusing on an obstacle to focusing on where we want to go is relatively simple to understand in biological terms. Humans are a complex mix of *perceptions*, information filtered through our past experiences, and *emotions*, subconscious reactions to our internal and external worlds. This interaction between perceptions and emotions influences our *physiology* or the metabolic processes that occur within the body. You may recall from high school biology that the end game of this constant fluctuation in physiology is an attempt to maintain *homeostasis*, the ideal operating range of our physical being. What does this mean in plain English? We love comfort and this biological process is all about finding the sweet spot where we can feel comfortable.

Our thoughts and feelings boil down to a *nervous system*, billions of neurons in the brain and other tissues in the body that first takes in information, then reacts metabolically, through neurotransmitters and hormones, to maintain balance. Our past experiences can create adaptations in the nervous system that can keep us stuck in high alert, and others that help us to return to calm. As you may have guessed, in the modern world many of us are wired for high alert. But we still have the capacity within us to return to calm. It is just a question of how to access these neural experiences and then allow them to spread to greater territory within our bodymind.

This process of purposefully rewiring the nervous system has been practiced on our planet for millennia. However, few people in the West actually know how to do this. The beauty is that rewiring happens naturally through what we term in modern science as *neural plasticity*, or the ability of networks in the brain and nervous system to change in response to our experiences. Spoiler alert: our survival instinct is also part of the wiring in our nervous system.

NEUROPLASTICITY WORKS

In the realm of practical application, when we practice a new thought pattern, the new experience replaces the old. The old experiences are still there, but the brain has a wonderful mechanism of *long-term depression* or "forgetting" memories that aren't important to us anymore. Through this process neurons within a certain network stop firing and over time the connection withers away. Which is great news if we wish to update our perceptual database! How might this work to our advantage?

You may have noticed that some folks are easy-going, while others are easily angered, and yet others are worried about everything under the sun. But what you may not know is that these are all practiced habit patterns. If we practice being angry, then we become angrier. If we practice being compassionate then we become more compassionate. This simple yet profound awareness can allow us to begin to take steps to mold our own nervous systems into something that we can be comfortable with. That's right, no matter what has happened in our past, we can purposefully rewire our nervous system through the choices that we make in our present.

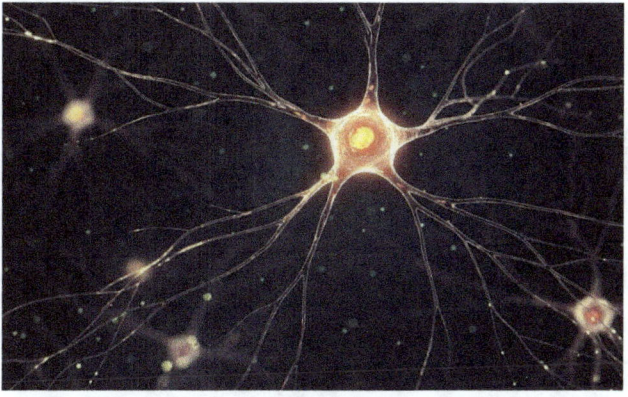

Neurons wiring through repeated activation and unwiring through deactivation. Image generated by Google Gemini, 2025.

Earlier I told you that the methods discussed in this book will change your life as they have mine. For example, my past tendency to explode at the smallest inconvenience has shifted to a comfort level within me and with those around me that no longer necessitates this behavior. We will discuss these methods for transformation at length in the following pages. Interestingly, this progression is often noticed more quickly by others than we can notice in ourselves. A few months into my journey a good friend from business school put it this way, "I don't know what you're doing but keep doing it. Man, you're different!"

THE BRAIN-BODY CONNECTION

One of the most important concepts for creating our own paths to well-being is that our thoughts and behaviors have physiological consequences. Our inner world impacts vital human functions such as heart rate, breathing, digestion, immune function, and sexual reproduction. In short, our perceptions and emotions directly impact our physical and mental health.

Although a late payment is stressful, it is typically not a life-threatening event. But your brain and body may respond as if your life were in danger. If we consider *stress* as a physical reaction to something threatening in our environment, then we might get curious about what actually happens to us within our physical bodies when we're stressed. When we experience a threat, our nervous system will choose the best course of action for survival. Current literature defines these subconscious strategies as fight/flight, freeze, and tend/befriend. Let's begin with the freeze response.

When we experience *freeze*, the nervous system goes into energy conservation mode, which can range from literally being frozen or catatonic to the point where we cannot move, to perhaps just feeling like we have zero energy and cannot get out of bed in the morning. Tend and befriend or the *fawn* state is similarly a lower energy state marked by nurturing behaviors. You have probably heard of the *fight or flight* response where the body and brain mobilize for action to either fight the perpetrator or flee from the scene: the pupils dilate, the heart pounds, and stress hormones flood the body. As we fight the enemy or run from

PRACTICE PAUSE: SOMETHING WONDERFUL

Let's try a brief experiment together.

Think back to a time when you were experiencing something wonderful in your life. Perhaps a new job or falling in love for the first time.

Sit with this for a moment and notice what the memory feels like in your body. What other thoughts are coming up for you? Did the weather or traffic bother you at this time in your life? What was your overall view of the world?

Now, think of a slightly uncomfortable experience, like scoring poorly on an important test, or missing a payment to the bank.

Sit with this for a moment and notice what the memory feels like in your body. What other thoughts are coming up for you? Did the weather or traffic bother you at this time? How did you feel about the world around you during this period?

Which experience do you prefer, thinking about something wonderful or something uncomfortable?

danger, we expend energy, stress hormones are metabolized through activity and there is a natural re-balancing of the nervous system. However, this calming restoration process does not happen when we get stressed and then just sit there. Stress hormones continue to circulate in the body, our muscles remain tense, and yes, we continue to worry about the situation, perpetuating this state of high alert.

Our magnificent brain is now working against us through the process of thinking about all the things that we cannot control. This physiological process is known as the *excessive stress response* and the harmful consequences that come with it are now well recognized in medical literature as stress related illnesses that include, among others, autoimmune diseases, cardiovascular disease, diabetes, and cancer. So, what can we do differently? We can move the body, exert energy, releasing the tension stored in the muscles, increasing blood flow and oxygen to the cells, and in essence complete the physiological action necessary to return to balance. Movement is critical to releasing stress in the bodymind!

For simplicity's sake, imagine that your brain has multiple superhighways of nerve connections. There are specific *neural pathways*, or circuits in the brain, responsible for executing survival processes in the body. I am now going to throw a few anatomical terms at you. Don't worry, you will not be tested on these later! But I do want you to understand these very important parts of the brain that relate to each of our individual experiences of the world.

The limbic system or threat circuit in the brain consists of the *amygdala*, the emotional sentinel, and the *hypothalamus*, the command center. They work together to create *homeostasis* or physiological balance. The amygdala receives information from our internal neural pathways, such as a knot in the stomach, as well as, the external environment, such as the late payment notice. These threats to our safety then activate the *hypothalamic-pituitary-adrenal* (HPA) axis that causes the release of stress hormones, such as, *cortisol*. Sounds like this could be problematic. But wait, there's more!

The amygdala is also part of the brain circuitry for moving emotional memories from short-term into long-term storage. And you guessed it. The stronger an emotional experience, the stronger the activation in the amygdala, and the greater the likelihood that this memory will be stored for future reference. This is a good thing if we want to store information critical to our survival, like the intersection where we witnessed a car accident yesterday. But a not-so-good thing if we *ruminate* or continue to replay a memory long after it happened, like *replaying* the car accident that happened 10 years ago.

When we are fed, rested, and experience a manageable level of stress, we typically have attention to expend on projects outside of daily survival. However, when stress begins to build, the survival network can become dominant and all our psychic energy, creative or otherwise, is overridden by the more important business of staying alive.

In my experience, this physiological process is most obvious when I consider myself in relation to others. For example, I may be having a conversation with someone, but my mind is elsewhere. When I ruminate on an old worry rather than focusing on the person or conversation, I lose the ability to be present with others. But how can stress factor into our ability to pay attention to the outer world? When we are stressed, we miss simple details and make mistakes that can lead to even more stressful situations.

There have been periods in my life when money was tight. I recall one instance when I needed a set amount of money in the bank to pay rent, so I carefully watched my expenses to keep the checking balance above this number. In this state of limbic system activation, or survival mode, I somehow managed to pay not one but TWO credit card bills twice! This sent my heartrate through the roof and created even more unnecessary worry and sleepless nights. These survival circuits are very different from the calm, rational planning circuits, or executive function. In this instance executive function was offline, and I was in survival mode. Some may call this forgetfulness, but my brain was so focused on the obstacle, lack of funds, that I lost the ability to see the path, like only paying my bills once.

Another peril is that when under stress, we can get into a cycle of distraction-seeking to temper our experiences of both actual events in the outer world and those imagined in the mind. What types of distraction seeking activities? Those that are rewarding to our brains! For instance, activities that distract us like movies, shopping, or scrolling social media, trigger a dopamine reward in the brain and are prime real estate in which to place our attention during stressful times. Which is great, up to a point. The problem is when this coping strategy begins to interfere with our ability to function in daily life, as illustrated in the following case studies.

SOCIAL MEDIA ADDICTION

Dan is a college professor who desires to achieve tenure at his university. He is doing research with a non-profit and has a full life of teaching, personal development, and community service. He regularly meditates but anxiety is a recurring phenomenon, not only in his meditation, but also in daily life. Dan often wonders why he feels so flustered and behind the eight-ball on work and important projects. I asked Dan how much time he spends on social media, and he exclaimed that "no one has time for that!" I then asked Dan to keep a log of time spent on social media for scientific measurement, and to note when and where he *used* social media and for what purpose.

It turns out that Dan cumulatively spends around two hours per day scrolling various social media platforms. Let's put this into perspective. Two hours per day is the equivalent of fourteen hours per week and fifty-six hours per month! In the morning Dan scans news outlets to keep up with world events, but he also noted that he watched TikTok for entertainment while brushing his teeth.

Through observation, Dan discovered that he kept his phone near him throughout the day and frequently picked up the phone to ping-pong between different social media platforms to keep up with world events, connect with friends, and for entertainment purposes. At night he would again, spend another 30-45 minutes scrolling various social media platforms.

Dan also discovered that he rarely focused on one task at a time. Rather he would begin to answer an email and then pick up his phone to again check social media. He also began to suspect that this constant multitasking wasn't helping his progression on the things that he wanted to finish each day. Dan is correct! The brain is good at executing one task at a time and when we have multiple choices before us, the brain is forced to choose, often leading to unpleasant experiences such as procrastination and anxiety.

Dan's wife was not surprised by our discovery that two hours were spent daily on social media. She suspected it was more like four hours. She reports, "He lives on his phone. When we get into the car, he gets on his phone. When we get to a restaurant and sit down together, the phone comes out. His attention is squarely focused on getting to that phone as quickly and as frequently as possible." Dan did not like comparing his social media use to addiction, but when I asked him to put down his phone for one hour each day, he reported that he could not do it. Furthermore, Dan could not believe that he spent two hours on social media each day. This phenomenon is known as *time distortion*, which is a prevalent experience in Social Media addicts. But how did Dan get into this predicament where he was no longer in control of his ability to focus on what he wanted to put energy into?

Let us start with a bold statement—there is one clear connection between human behavior and our deteriorating health and well-being. It is stress. What kind of stress are we talking about? In lay terms we will begin with the term *chronic stress*, or a persistent activation of the limbic system. A little later in this book we will delve into the realm of *traumatic stress*.

How big of a deal is stress in modern society? The American Psychological Association collects annual data on the impact of stress in the United States and the latest survey suggests that we are in a stress induced crisis. This is not just a challenge in the United States. Around the globe, humans are not effectively managing stress, which is leading to an epidemic of mental and physical disease. There are even more maladaptive coping strategies that many of us rely upon to manage stress.

COMFORT FOOD ADDICTION

Jerry is an educator, father, and stress researcher. He knows all about the physiology behind stress eating, and yet he keeps two sets of clothes in the closet, the extra-large size for stressful periods of life and the large ones for when life is more manageable. How many of us utilize this same coping strategy, and keep one pair of comfy pants on hand, just in case? Why do we eat food that is unhealthy for us, even when we know better? There are several theories. Some research suggests it is about social modeling; repeating the behavior of what other people in our social circles do. But many of us crave sugary or salty foods, without a clear explanation. It might surprise you to know that the body craves these foods when under stress and eating these foods reduces the stress hormone cortisol.

Those of us with access to fast food have intuitively used this quick and easy stress management tool, albeit one with potentially devastating consequences. Furthermore, the food science industries create products with the express purpose of keeping us hooked. Food chemists are in the business of devising snacks that create craving, without satiety, which leads to over indulging, obesity, and subsequent health problems.

ALCOHOL ADDICTION

Many of the maladaptive coping strategies that we adopt to deal with stress can begin in early childhood. Escaping through food, or various forms of entertainment are often modeled by parental figures or age peers as coping strategies. For many young people, the modeled behavior is alcohol use. Eileen began using alcohol to deal with challenging emotions in her early teens. As a young person she would drink to feel normal and comfortable around other people.

Her home life, punctuated by abusive caregivers, contributed to her nervous system remaining stuck in fight or flight. Over the years Eileen found that alcohol was the one method that she could count on for relief from the uncertainty of her childhood home. More tragically, alcohol was the one thing that she began to look forward to each day. As a teen, she hid a bottle of alcohol in her room for easy access when she felt overwhelmed. As an adult, she could not wait to get to a restaurant and order a bottle of wine or make it home to her nightly martini. Unfortunately, these brief and contrived moments of respite came at a high cost.

One fateful evening, after consuming a fair amount of alcohol, she was driving home from a party. A woman in a muscle car lurched her car to get ahead of Eileen's car at a merge. Without hesitation, Eileen lurched to cut her off, at which point the other driver gunned her car to cut in front, missing Eileen's car by inches. Both drivers exited the merge separated only by rubber pylons. The driver of the muscle car made a few inflammatory hand gestures, and before Eileen knew what happened, she had driven her car across the lane, crunching a line of rubber pylons and crashing into the front quarter panel of the other driver's car. Eileen had rammed her car into another person's car, without any conscious awareness of what had just happened.

Eileen had no understanding that the limbic or emotional network in the brain had overridden her thinking network and that she was operating in a physiological survival response. Nor did she understand how alcohol excites the threat driven amygdala and suppresses the calm, rational prefrontal cortex. But what she did understand was that her drinking was now dangerously impacting other parts of her life. And more importantly, this incident created an urgent need for an effective set of tools to manage her subconscious rage.

These three case studies illustrate how it may seem natural to soothe ourselves through activities that make us feel better, but any activity that triggers a dopamine reward in the brain creates a cycle of learning that, "This is something that we would like to do more of," and if we get a big enough push of "That feels good," then the reward circuits of the brain will ask for more. Simple pleasures like scrolling for a few minutes on social media, or enjoying a little extra junk food, or maybe a couple of alcoholic beverages are the exact neurological processes in which a little bit of soothing can slowly amplify into a problematic behavior.

So, what can we do about this physiological conundrum? I have wonderful news for you! Just like other aspects of our biology, the nervous system is malleable. Imagine a cell that can change course and actually connect to a different cell in the body. That's exactly what a neuron can do. Behold the magical power of your nervous system!

TIME TO REWIRE

This remarkable biological design consists of gaps between *neurons* and *synapses* or chemical and electrical impulses that jump from neuron to neuron across these gaps. The information flowing from each cell within your brain and body are these synapses. New connections are created through repetition of a thought or action.

Let's say that you decide to place your attention on playing the piano. In the beginning you have little control over which key that you hit with a finger and limited ability to coordinate the left and right hand, but with consistent practice, new connections are made between nerve cells in the muscles in your hand, motor neurons leading from the hand to the brain, and the *motor cortex* in your brain. With time and practice viola! This is the process by which you can progress from playing Chopsticks to Chopin.

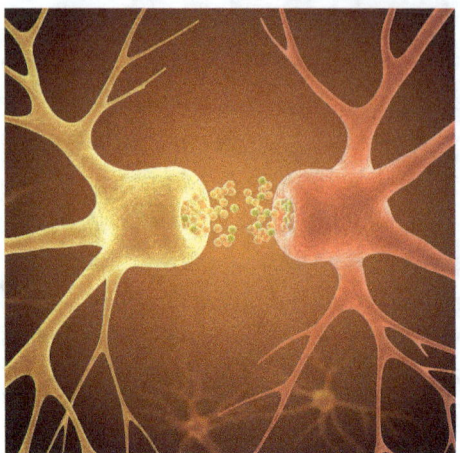

Neurons Firing, Wiring, and Waiting for New Connections. Image generated by Google Gemini, 2025.

Our thoughts are part of this circuitry that with practice, we can bring into awareness, and make changes that influence the entire physiology of the body. Therefore, we are not biologically hardwired to behave the same way day after day. Thanks to this process of *neuroplasticity* or repeat after me, "neurons that fire together wire together" we possess an ability to strengthen whatever network in the brain that we wish to enhance, by focusing on that specific type of thought or behavior.

If we view the brain as an ever-changing organ that learns through experiences, then a better question is, what can we do to enhance our ability to choose wisely? This is where Chris' advice to "Focus on your path, not the obstacles" comes to life. Repetition of any thought, action, or behavior will wire into a well-worn path in our nervous system. When we worry about what is out of our control or the unknown, we are focusing on the obstacles and strengthening those circuits in the brain that create even more confusion. And when we choose positive thoughts, actions, or behaviors, a new path will emerge, and unwanted behaviors will wither over time.

I set an intention to apply this information to my own bodymind transformation. Neuroplasticity made perfect sense to me in theory, but life is messy. I thought to myself, how on earth can I control the world to create beneficial experiences for neuroplasticity to occur?

After a good laugh I decided that the only logical practice would be to use any and every experience in life as an opportunity to grow. The sage Shantideva posed this question, "Is it easier to cover the world in leather or to put on a pair of shoes"? I now understand that I cannot control conditions in the external world, but I can put on a pair of shoes and thereby learn to temper my reactions to whatever situations I encounter during daily life.

THE BIG LIFE QUESTIONS

As a researcher I knew that I needed to translate this intention into a testable question. I now had two clear and practical research questions in mind:

Is there a method to experience life in such a way that calmer pathways in the brain are strengthened?

Is it possible to rewire the nervous system from survival-based circuits to rational thought pathways?

These research questions informed my mission in life. Through constant trial and error in various situations I have begun to embrace the art of living through focusing on where I want to go regardless of the obstacles I face. Chris' words became part of my own guiding principle. With time I discovered that when I chose resting in a calm body and mind, where I wanted to go, rather than focusing on the obstacles, what could go wrong, it was not only easier to find solutions to daily dilemmas, but often a path to these solutions would emerge that I had not even considered!

Through continued meditation, observation and introspection practice I gained an ability to transfer what I learned on the meditation cushion into daily life, to view whatever was happening in front of me through the eyes of an observer. The more objectivity that came, the greater the access to understanding my own behaviors. It was as if I had graduated from preschool and was now ready for a new level of learning. One thing was evident, I had hit another wall. I desperately wanted to keep growing and, therefore, I would need to delve into other forms of exploration to continue this experiment.

A gentle reminder. Mt. Baden-Powell Trailhead. Photo Credit: R. K. Rodgers

CHAPTER 4

THE PATH APPEARS

By my early 40s, I was ready for extreme change, and was willing to up the game and get deeper into meditation. I looked for meditation resources on the Internet and found a treasure trove of audio, video, and written words to help soothe the racing thoughts in my mind. I learned that there are two general meditation methods, one where we give the mind something to do, *focused attention meditation*, like breath counting and one where we open ourselves to everything in our environment, so we can notice what our mind is up to outside of conscious attention, *open awareness meditation*.

As a seeker of new experiences, I decided to experiment with both techniques. When the mind was racing, I found it helpful to have something to focus upon during meditation practice. This could be a sound, like my own breath, birds chirping outside my window, or the voice of a teacher leading me through a guided meditation. When my mind was less tumultuous, I experimented with being an observer of the "show" going on in the projector of my mind, not judging the show, just noticing how quickly these vignettes would arise and float away or morph into other thoughts, scenarios, or flights of fantasy about people, places, and events from the past or the future.

Many of the guided meditations started with the instruction to close the eyes, which for me was tricky. Some days I could comfortably close my eyes and others it made me feel claustrophobic. If the goal was to quiet the mind, then worrying about the walls closing in was certainly not helping. I made the decision to do whatever would help me to remain in meditation a little longer during each session. I often sat with eyes open, focused on the floor just in front of me. This would help to minimize the distractions of scanning the room visually, while giving me a level of comfort in keeping my eyes open.

These practices were a great start, but I felt as if I needed more information to understand the intricacies of the meditation experience. As I became open to this possibility, I found a small shop in Claremont, California that had exotic statues in the window. I entered the shop and found a woman named Barb sitting in a plastic lawn chair. She had a gentle Southern accent, was warm and kind, and I had the strange sense that we knew each other somehow. I told her that I was going through a big transition and needed help finding my way. I was leaving a marriage, a job, a city, and everything that defined my existence. She went straight to the shelf and pulled down *The Places That Scare You: A Guide to Fearlessness in Difficult Times* by Pema Chödrön (2007). I laughed and mentioned how nice it was for this person to write a book about my life. Barb assured me that she had read the book while facing similar obstacles and that if she could do it, then so could I.

I took the book home and carefully began to dissect each page. I learned about the concept of *bodhichitta*, or awakened heart, the practice of opening our hearts to the pain that surrounds us, softening into the experiences of life. I had spent my entire life battling my environment, stuffing emotions, and running from pain. It never occurred to me that this was only prolonging my suffering. I had also been raised with the concept of an "eye for an eye," which only breeds more hatred and violence rather than promoting healing. It also defies the love that each of us have deep within us. If we want a different outcome in our modern world, then we need a completely different orientation to ourselves and fellow beings, which is bodhichitta.

This book also helped to clarify the purpose of meditation, which is to experience ourselves just as we are. I had hoped that meditation would be a non-stop feel-good fest. However, often the exact opposite would occur. My mind would race with myriad thoughts, or the sensations in my body would be so intense that I would abruptly end the meditation and jump to something less distressing. I now understand that all of this is a necessary part of practice.

I believed that I was a broken human that needed repair, and that meditation would help to fix me. Once I came to understand that each of us, at our core, are imbued with goodness, then I found hope that I might tap into this goodness that lies within. We each possess an inner wisdom which we can rely upon for direction. Meditation helps us to connect with this vital part of ourselves.

How could Pema, a Buddhist nun, know these things? How could she be so calm after enduring such hardship in her own life? As with *Siddhartha*, which had been a source of strength so many years ago, this book stoked my passion for Buddhism. But I now focused on using this information for living rather than for escaping life when times were tough.

I was developing greater awareness of my inner world and the rote behaviors that I had relied upon for so many years began to disintegrate. As I shifted on the inside, the outside kept pace. Synchronicities began to occur, and it seemed as if I would bump into just the right person at the right time.

As my mind became more settled, a positive chain of events began to spring forth from these ever-expanding periods of calmness, clarity, and spontaneous connections. For example, one afternoon I felt drawn to attend a mixer at my business school and a random person approached me to chat. We struck up a conversation about suffering in the workplace and how corporate culture often creates an atmosphere of constant fear and panic. I told him how I wanted to find a different way of doing business and life. He asked if I was familiar with the concept of *flow*, which he described as being in tune with the present moment and moving effortlessly with our surrounding circumstances. I had no idea of such a concept. He then recommended I read *Flow* by Mihaly Csikszentmihalyi (1990) to see if this information might be helpful. I purchased the book that evening, skimmed the first few pages, then put it down without much thought.

I was in the middle of a divorce and slept an hour or two per night; I was a zombie, relying on caffeine, Ibuprofen, and alcohol to get me through the day. My mind was elsewhere, to put it mildly. Days later I had *Flow* at the top of a pile of books, sitting on my table at the local coffee shop. A stranger approached me and said "This is an amazing book, don't you think? I had difficulty getting through the second chapter, but after I worked through it, this book changed my life!" The stranger disappeared; I opened the book and found a bookmark on the last page of the second chapter. Dear friends, within a period of two weeks I had been approached by two complete strangers encouraging me to read the same book. How often do we get such clear directions in life without paying attention?

I began to pay attention to these directions that were becoming more common, directions that were guiding me, and that I had previously lacked awareness to notice. I read *Flow* again from the beginning, this time placing my undivided attention into the book and absorbing every word. The next piece of vital information in this journey appeared on the page, "To control attention is to control quality of life." My attention was all over the place and unbridled thoughts were destroying my quality of life!

Through meditation I was learning to slow down the chatter in my mind and to direct attention to more positive aspects of life. It was so simple, yet so profound. My mind had until recently spun a whirlwind of negative thoughts, which had led to chaos in my inner world. All the programming from childhood, my career, and home life were now well-worn habit patterns keeping me stuck in misery. *Flow* provided me with the insight that it was up to ME to change these thoughts and patterns of behavior. And this, my friends, is the way that we change our reality and our lives. We must begin to notice our thoughts to determine which reality we are creating. I will say this in a different way. What you practice, you get good at. So, when we practice negative thinking, we get good at it, which leads to the thoughts and emotions that create a negative outcome. And therefore, thanks to neuroplasticity, as we think, so we become.

Although I had only been meditating for a short while, I quickly realized this practice was a direct gateway to change. Through meditation I was coming to certain realizations about subconscious behaviors. I discovered that whenever I felt uncomfortable, I would run toward a distraction, such as shopping for something that I thought would bring me happiness, grab a coffee, a cocktail, or look for some form of entertainment to escape the sensations and emotions that were coming up.

EXERCISE: DISTINGUISHING
MEDITATION FROM RUMINATION

The practice of meditation is one method to create more space in an overcrowded mind. However, we must honestly assess if our time is spent meditating or if we are allowing our minds to run wild. If this is the case, then we are not practicing meditation; we are reinforcing the thought patterns that keep the nervous system activated.

Set a timer for 5 minutes

Set an intention at the beginning of this meditation session to practice with a purpose.

Notice any thoughts that arise and then release them. We don't try to stop the thoughts, but rather gain an awareness of how often thoughts arise. If you find yourself thinking throughout your meditation session then remember that this is counterproductive to your goal.

Refresh your intention to practice with a purpose.

Observe this process of thoughts arising and ceasing.

Gaining awareness of what the mind is up to.

Every moment of stillness of mind is a step in the right direction.

For instance, during meditation an uncomfortable sensation would arise and suddenly I remembered that I had an email to answer. Did I need to answer the email at that exact moment? No! But my mind insisted that I get up and take care of this "important" task right away.

I sincerely wanted to bring calm into my daily experience, but sitting and focusing on my breath was bringing up all sorts of scheming in my mind. It was as if this process of watching my thoughts was creating a rift between the new calm spaces within me and the old tumultuous storm so familiar to my nervous system.

For many of us this chaotic space is very familiar and, therefore, moving into new territory can be uncomfortable. But that is just what we must do if we are to be successful in finding peace. We must develop our bodhichitta, awakening heart, to become comfortable with the experience of just being in our skin, no matter which thoughts or sensations arise.

I had developed some confidence in my daily meditation practice and felt ready to move to the next level. A dear friend suggested that I try a ten-day meditation retreat to explore the internal conflict that I was experiencing during meditation.

MY FIRST MEDITATION RETREAT

I am off to once-and-for-all calm my chaotic mind. A trip to Joshua Tree in the Mojave Desert will be just the ticket to find the peace that I seek. My friend recommended an exciting type of meditation called *Vipassana*, a profound therapy formulated in India centuries ago by Shakyamuni Buddha. This was the medicine available before painkillers, psychiatric medication, and talk therapy. As someone with a tendency to overreact to threats in the environment, Vipassana could help me to divide reality into what is there versus what I perceive through the window of my own experiences. My goal was to dig into the thoughts that troubled me and perhaps rid them from the deepest parts of my bodymind. Great!

The first day we learned the basics of *Ānāpānasati*, a mindfulness of breathing technique. The 60 or so fellow retreatants and I then practiced in the meditation hall for two days, slowly building up attention, so that later in the retreat we could practice sitting for an hour without moving a muscle. Strangely, we built our attention by focusing on one part of the body, the nose. The instruction was simple enough; we were asked to notice the sensations around the nostrils as we breathed in and out.

This may seem rather boring and pointless, and at first, I could feel nothing: no air coming in or out, no heat or coolness, nor any sensations at all, and I assumed that this was normal. I did not really put much energy into what my mind was up to because I was focused so hard on trying to feel the sensations in my nose that the teacher kept speaking about, tickling, itching, warmth, and coolness.

This went on for three days, hour after hour, just sitting and putting effort into noticing the sensations around my nostrils as I breathed. Days later it occurred to me that the act of focusing so intensely on sensations was also helping to quiet the racing thoughts. My mind was single-pointedly fixated on sensations, so not much else was happening with internal thought processes.

One evening as I sat in my dorm room, practicing Ānāpānasati, it was as if someone flipped a sensation switch in my brain. I suddenly had awareness of thousands of tingles all over my body. I could now notice what I had been missing for years, the sensations of the smallest increment of movement on my skin. My mind could experience warm air coming into my nostrils and cool air exiting my nostrils. I suddenly noticed that my throat was dry and there was a slight breeze moving beneath my knees. Most noticeable was the knot of muscles between my eyebrows. How long had my forehead been locked in this worried position? I was in wonder at this sudden ability to feel sensations all over my body. I now understand that this was a crucial part of the journey to reconnect body and mind. Without an awareness of sensorial experiences, I could not begin to untangle the knots such as the one between my eyebrows.

Now you may be asking how I could not feel the sensations in my body and perhaps if I had a neurological disorder. I could feel gross sensations in the body, like aching shoulders or a migraine headache, but I could not feel the subtle sensations like tingling in my feet or a knot in my eyebrows. This is not a neurological limitation, but rather a lack of refinement in mental attention. I had purposefully disconnected from my body by staying lost in thoughts, some of the past, some of the future, some of just wants and not wants. For instance, I knew that I wanted a Dr. Pepper in the worst way, and I did not want to place my attention on these newfound sensations. But I was intrigued with this rush of information, so I went forward with the next step in the Vipassana process, noticing thoughts as they arise and then returning my focus to the sensations of the breath.

The first three days of the retreat are dedicated to Ānāpānasati, and it took every bit of this time to accomplish the slightest bit of ability in the practice. I was warned that my body might protest the lack of stimulation and the immense effort that is expended in focused attention on the breath. This was an understatement.

It was day four of the retreat and I could wrestle my mind periodically from a stream of thoughts to the sensations of the breath leaving my nose for successively longer periods. It was now 10-20-30 seconds before the next thought would pop into awareness. You may be thinking, yeah, but this is normal, thoughts come and go. I once had the same opinion, but my thoughts would never shut off. They ran constantly, during meetings at work, during conversations with loved ones, and late into the night as I desperately tried to sleep. I now understood that my mind was malfunctioning and began to suspect that this was instrumental in the implosions of my career, relationships, and health.

As the days went by, we progressively sat for longer periods of time, at first 15, then 20, then 30 minutes. I was told that tomorrow we will sit for one hour in complete stillness and silence to develop *Adhiṭṭhāna*, a strong determination. Previously my longest sit in silence was 30 minutes, but I was determined to do this hour-long sit perfectly, and so I made a pact with myself that it would happen.

The morning came and there I sat in the meditation hall wiggling, squirming, feeling pain in places I had never noticed before. The meditation bell rang, and thanks to my newfound friend "sensations" I quickly noticed that my head was pulsing, my knees were throbbing, and my back ached.

The pain in my body added another layer of chatter in my overcrowded mind. I worried that I would not be able to make the one-hour goal and began to wonder how long I had been sitting there. Was it five or ten minutes, or maybe closer to half an hour? *Great! Only 30 minutes left!* But wait, what if I was wrong and I still had 45 minutes left? How would I endure this pain for 45 more minutes? And this went on for some time: worrying, wiggling, squirming, worrying, and occasionally remembering to breathe. Again, and again, I would listen to the meditation instructions while watching my inner terror grow exponentially with each passing minute.

I knew that I was a strong person. I had never missed a day of work. I am a determined person. I completed a business degree while working a 50-hour week! I had muscled my way through many obstacles in life. Clearly, I could do this. I went back to the sensations of the breath at the nostrils. But then my heart started pounding faster, I felt nauseated and could feel breakfast coming up in my throat, I opened my eyes, and the room was spinning. A profuse sweat ran down my face and soaked my shirt. I wanted to run for the door but knew that if I tried to stand up, I would pass out. I breathed deeply and surrendered to what would come next. Either I would vomit or faint or some combination of the two, but one thing was clear, this was beyond my control, and I would have to ride it out.

I choked breakfast back down, continued to breathe deeply, and eventually the ending bell rang. I stood slowly and made my way back to the dorms. I was feeling better and thought perhaps no one had noticed what happened back in the meditation hall. I entered my room and looked in the mirror. My shirt and hair were drenched! It literally looked like I had run through a fire hydrant. Just then there was a knock on the door. Someone said, "Are you okay? We thought we might have to call 911!"

I replied, "Yes, I'm okay." But clearly, I was not okay. I had no idea what had happened. Was it something I ate? Was it a panic attack? What the hell!?

I was beyond confused. I am strong and determined. This sort of thing does not happen to me! I spoke with the assistant teacher later that day to ask what to do next. She explained that this was common for beginners to Vipassana meditation. She said, "When we begin to reconnect body and mind, we make the mind uncomfortable, and the body reacts." This made some sense to me, but I was still shaken by the fact that my body reacted without direction from my mind. Until today, I believed that my mind ran the show, and the body was a faithful servant. But today my body acted out as my mind watched helplessly. Another thing troubled me. I was in a room full of 60 other human beings of all ages, genders, ethnicities, and to my knowledge, no one else in the room had this type of reaction. Was I really that screwed up? What was so different about me?

As it turned out, this may have just been a brief meditative experience, also known as *nyam*. Any number of pleasant or unpleasant experiences can arise during practice: paranoia, fear, bliss, and everything in between. When we make the time to work with our minds, our bodies may sometimes participate in the rebellion. But these experiences, as with everything in life, are impermanent. That's the good news! No matter how intense the sensations or thoughts are, they will dissipate with time. The important thing is not to privilege and repeat this experience, let it come up and pass, and then we return to the practice. It is also important to seek help when we encounter these intense experiences, so we can understand the causes and conditions of our discomfort and find a way to move through them. That is what I decided to do. I sought help so I could grow through this experience, rather than run from it.

Mt. Lukens Trailhead, Glendale, CA.
Photo Credit: R.K. Rodgers

THE THINGS WE DON'T TALK ABOUT AND OFTEN DON'T KNOW

I am no different than any other free roaming human who is not incarcerated or institutionalized. I was knocked around as a kid, but hey, who wasn't, right? I was raised in the South where this was life, and you'd better just toughen up and face the facts. This was my impression of childhood, and as far as I could tell, I was not alone.

I grew up on a diet of salty fried foods, Dr. Pepper, and Country Music. Conventional wisdom was that any problem could be solved by a glass of whiskey or a tall stranger next to the jukebox. This worked for me for a long while—until it didn't. My meditation retreat experience gave me a glimpse of a different reality and I found that the things that I relied upon to get me through the day were making me miserable and sick.

Given my predicament I went to a medical doctor and asked for guidance. She told me to "lower my stress" as if I had any idea how to really do this. I asked for specifics. She said, "change your diet, get exercise, and slow down on smoking and drinking." But I had already tried these things, and I still had to take 10-12 Ibuprofen to make it through the aches and pains of the day, followed by a martini or two to get to sleep. My doctor was not at fault. She had been trained in a western medical school to western standards where the answer to every problem is a pill or surgery.

I went back to her after some months of powering through my suffering and she once again told me to lower my stress, but this time she offered sleeping pills to solve my sleepless nights. My mind flashed to parents who had been prescribed a cocktail of medications for the past four decades. For me this was not an option, and I knew that I had to find a different way. A way that broke from the tradition of alcohol and sleeping pills, as well as, the endless self-abuses that had brought me to this point in life. I kindly declined the sleeping pills, and my doctor then suggested that I see a therapist. I reacted strongly to this suggestion because my mother had been in therapy for decades and, in my opinion, this had yielded less than optimal results. But I had run out of options, so I did the unthinkable. I called a therapist.

TALK THERAPY

My first conversation with a Marriage and Family Therapist was over the phone. She introduced herself and sounded like a pleasant enough person. I in return needed her to know up front that prescription drugs were not an option for me. She explained that she was not a psychiatrist and had no desire to put me on drugs and, furthermore, she had no plans at all. She was there to guide me to wherever I wished to go. She also suggested that we take it one session at a time, and I could leave whenever I wanted, no pressure. The therapist had calmed me to the point of willingness, so I agreed to come in for an office visit.

The visit was going well, and she seemed nice enough as we began with intake information: age, education, background, relationship status. And then she asked me why I was there. I told her that I needed to lower my stress. I was in the midst of a painful divorce and probably the whole cause of this mess was that I was a workaholic. She nodded, took some notes, and then went straight to the first inquiry, "So, tell me about your mother." I was aghast! How cliché! What a waste of time! This session had turned into a parody of every skit about a therapist I had seen in my life. Clearly this woman could not help me, and I was ready to bolt out the door.

She sensed the chaos going on in my mind and assured me that this was just to get a better idea of my background history. I thought that sounded reasonable, so I calmed down. The interview continued and minute by minute I grew easier with the process of talking about my past in search of a better future. A few sessions went by and it became clear that my childhood relationships had a lot to do with my discomfort with the world. The therapist said that we each have an attachment style based upon how we as small, helpless creatures were nurtured or neglected. In early life, we are at the mercy of our caregivers for food, water, shelter, and emotional support. It turns out that a child who was nurtured and made to feel safe goes through life very differently than one who was neglected, abandoned or abused.

A colleague, George Haas, who teaches meditation-based attachment theory explained it this way, "People that are securely attached to a caregiver have no idea how scary the world is for those of us who are insecurely attached." If you have no idea what I am talking about, good for you! You dodged a bullet. But for those of us who live life constantly scanning our environment for the next landmine, you may want to explore attachment theory further. A wonderful book on the topic is *The Power of Attachment: How to Create Deep and Lasting Intimate Relationships* by Diane Poole Heller, Ph.D. (2019).

The therapist referred to my condition as *the parenting child*, someone who must grow up quickly to assume responsibility for their own safety and oftentimes their parent or caregiver's safety as well. This behavior, learned early in life, follows us year after year and relationship after relationship.

With this knowledge, *puzzle piece number one* came into focus. I now had awareness of my maladaptive orientation to the external world. I needed to control everything around me so I could feel safe. Unfortunately, this orientation toward life is not only impossible to manage, but also highly anxiety provoking. I will never control the weather, world events, traffic, or others' behaviors. What is in my control is how I interpret and react to these events.

This marked my first awareness of the need for releasing childhood patterns of fear, anger, and frustration. My perceptual database was that of a neglected child. It was time to update this database, to allow a more adaptive way of viewing people and circumstances around me to facilitate healthier adult behaviors.

To embark upon this journey, I had to move away from tracking the behaviors of others, their reactions and facial expressions, and begin seeking to understand my own behavior. In Vedic philosophy, this is an important part of growth known as *svaadhyaaya*, self-study, when one seeks to understand not only who we are, but also how we interact with other beings in our external world.

There was one other critical term that was introduced during our therapy sessions—*codependent*. As a small child I did everything I could to get my mother's attention. It is a biological survival strategy that over time can develop into an unhealthy obsession with worrying about the caregiver, while dealing with the uncertainty of one's own safety. These well-developed patterns from childhood had followed me into adult life, both in my career and in romantic relationships.

With time and more therapy, I slowly came to understand why I felt so unsafe in my own skin. My nervous system had become a worst-case-scenario manufacturing machine. It is difficult to connect with another human while in fight or flight, so my relationships were superficial shells of what could be. Similarly, I could not experience a moment of peace, for my world was a never-ending barrage of disaster planning and reactivity to these imaginary scenarios, that were oh so real in my body and mind.

Time passed, the divorce was finalized, and I continued searching for a better way of living. I was ready to abandon the notion that life would always be hard and that I just needed to toughen up to get through it. I now had information that I could use to make changes rather than masking the pain. Through all of this, I became fascinated with the mind-body connection and its influence on human behavior. I now had two major challenges before me. First, I had no idea how to create and sustain happiness in my own life and second, no one in my circle of friends or coworkers had advice outside of the "get a good job and nice relationship and everything will fall into place" model. I needed to find a solution to these challenges but had no idea where to look.

DISCOVERY

CHAPTER 5

WHEN THE STUDENT IS READY TEACHERS APPEAR

Better than a thousand days of diligent study is one day with a great teacher

—Japanese proverb

Therapy opened the door for me to explore new avenues to create calm in my life. I realized that I could no longer tolerate the fifty-hour work week, corporate lifestyle that I once believed was the key to happiness. I was desperate to learn more about lowering stress without distractions or medication. Then, of course, there were the ever-present research questions:

Is there a method to experience life in such a way that calmer pathways in the brain are strengthened?

Is it possible to rewire our nervous system from old fear-based survival circuits to new calm and rational thought pathways?

I needed training to bring these questions into a testable research program. I applied to and remarkably was accepted into Claremont Graduate University, the same school in which Mihaly Csikszentmihalyi, the author of *Flow*, taught courses. That remarkable book which had explained the connection between where we place our attention and our quality of life.

I dove headfirst into coursework that would enable me to learn more about the science of stress and hopefully discover a path to my own well-being. One pivotal class that I took during this discovery process was "The Practice of Self-Management" at the Drucker School. At this time, anger was my default emotion for most scenarios in life. I knew that I had a short fuse and what better way to continue healing than to learn and practice methods for addressing anger.

The professor, Jeremy Hunter, Ph.D., became a mentor and dear friend, and provided me with instruction on how to first notice and then later change challenging behavior patterns. I discovered that I spent a lot of time in worry and dread, which I masked with the emotion of anger. With this awareness, I could now work at the root of the problem, rather than just masking the symptoms. I also learned about the biology of stress and came to understand the difference between *a little* stress and long-term persistent *chronic* stress, which can contribute to coronary, digestive, reproductive, and autoimmune disorders that not surprisingly, when left unchecked will eventually kill us.

Jeremy introduced me to another person that would change my life, Elaine Miller-Karas, MSW, LCSW, cofounder of the Trauma Resource Institute (TRI). TRI is a critical, global health organization that sends trainers around the world to help those who have experienced traumas such as war and natural disaster. Trainers then share simple skills to rebalance the nervous system and regain mental and emotional composure, which survivors can use as a foundation to begin to rebuild their lives.

I had little understanding of the word trauma before meeting Elaine. In medical terms, we think of *trauma* as the result of some physical impact like what happens to the body when hitting a windshield at sixty miles per hour, but there is also a psychic element to trauma. For example, what traces of this experience are left in the nervous system after we hit the windshield? I soon came to learn that many of us are suffering from trauma without knowing it. It is not socially acceptable to talk about these things in most cultures, so we go along in life unaware that a good friend's son committed suicide, or another friend who served in Iraq ducks his head whenever driving under an overpass, although he is no longer in danger of decapitation in the turret of his Humvee.

Elaine taught me that *trauma* can manifest from a small event such as a bee sting, to what are typically considered major events like experiencing personal harm, or natural disaster, or witnessing others being harmed or abused. For some, trauma may manifest from an event that happened when they were not able to consciously register the event. For instance, trauma that happens to an infant, before the brain is fully developed, or to an adult during surgery while under anesthesia.

Others may endure the *cumulative trauma* of repeated exposure to aggressions such as living in an environment or culture that is not safe. Still others may experience trauma from the stacking effect of multiple challenging experiences over a long period.

The biological truth of the matter is that our own nervous systems determine what is or is not traumatic; trauma may not seem logical or proportional from another person's point of view. Therefore, trauma is not something to measure, rationalize, or compare to others. The key point is that if you experience an event as, "too much" or "too soon" for the nervous system to process, the bodymind can react with its protective mechanisms that will enable you to fight/flee, freeze, or tend/befriend (fawn). With this information, we are now ready to expand our definition of the *bodymind* as an integrated relationship between psychological and physiological processes within a human, as well as, the embodied manifestations of these processes.

THE T WORD

You may be thinking that trauma is not "your thing" or part of your story. I did too for many years. The mind takes care of us by blocking content from our past that may be too threatening to our present.

After someone experiences a traumatic event, the memory may be fragmented, making it difficult to bring into conscious awareness. While subconsciously, any multitude of sensory triggers can serve as reminders of this event, transporting the person back, as if the event were happening in the present moment (Miller-Karas, 2023). These *memory capsules* (Scaer, 2005) or multi-sensory reminders of a traumatic event, remain dormant until a sensory trigger sparks a release. Therefore, we must assume a *trauma-informed perspective* for our own healing, understanding that certain practices such as closing the eyes, deep breathing, or remaining still for periods of time, may trigger a memory capsule.

This is what happened when I naively jumped into an advanced meditation practice. My experience with Vipassana had done exactly what it was designed to do, uncover the stress and trauma stored in the bodymind. What I did not understand was that this experience could be too much for my nervous system, and probing into unconscious spaces could trigger a survival response.

During the intense experience in Vipassana meditation, I had been instructed to sit in stillness for one hour. This direction in itself was a type of physical constraint that threatened my sense of safety. I did have free will. I could have gotten up and left the hall, but I wanted to push through at all costs. This intense probing into the sensations in the body brought long buried subconscious material into the conscious realm. For me, this overwhelming experience in the meditation hall was too-much-too-soon and this is why I had the extreme experience of nausea, profuse sweating, and panic. Thanks to Vipassana and talk therapy, I was now in touch with the sensations of the body, and they were ready to share their stories.

SENSATION: THE GATEWAY TO AWARENESS

Much like learning to read a book, we must develop *body literacy*, observing sensations to decipher how felt experiences in the body can influence our thoughts, actions, and behaviors (Miller-Karas, 2023). As we develop this skill, we gain conscious access to subconscious information about past experiences (Gendlin, 2007) and create the opportunity to experience an embodied sense of well-being (Farb, 2015).

Imagine for a moment that you have a deep wound that appears normal on the surface, but continues to deteriorate beneath the skin. You may not be consciously aware of this damage, but subconsciously the bodymind is working nonstop on the injury. Your immune system is fighting damage at a cellular level, and survival pathways in the brain have made note of the causes and conditions that led to this injury, creating habits to avoid this type of event in the future. The same process extends beyond cuts and bruises, into the realm of psychological harm.

Vipassana meditation is one such process that can restore the feedback loop of information and bring it into our awareness, we can then create a space to release the energy behind the injury.

Vipassana restores our awareness of the sensations in the body and BAM! We notice the wound and all the accompanying distress associated with a problem that needs immediate attention. For this reason, Vipassana meditation can initially be an overwhelming experience for the nervous system. I say initially, because the point of Vipassana is to become aware of these sensations, and then observe how they are transient, coming and going, shifting from place to place, never stable. Once we become an observer of this process, then we can allow sensations and the accompanying thoughts, like *when will this ever end,* come and go as well.

There is an energetic quality to the events of the past that are buried in the body. It takes a lot of energy to stuff emotions and memories, and as we tap into these somatic records of the past, the energy may be released in dramatic ways: shaking, crying, screaming, and yes, even buckets of sweat. The challenge is that this type of awakening experience can be perceived as a threat. In my case I was able to recover from the overwhelming experience in a few minutes. For others, including those who may have experienced trauma, this challenge can extend beyond the initial momentary experience into months or years (Britton, et al, 2021). Therefore, therapies that involve delving into our internal world should be approached with a *trauma-informed lens,* an understanding and toolkit of best practices to assist those who have experienced trauma.

At the time of my first Vipassana retreat, I had zero knowledge of: memory capsules, the pitfalls of non-trauma informed practices, the processes behind regulation and dysregulation of the nervous system, nor the adverse reactions that can occur when an experience overwhelms our sense of safety. More importantly, I did not have the ability to recognize when my own nervous system was out of balance, nor did I have the tools to rebalance my nervous system as soon as distressing sensations arose.

It is fascinating that in modern society with an abundance of technological and scientific information, we have totally lost touch with our bodies, have difficulty controlling our minds, and have never been taught that we have the capacity to manage these systems.

I had also been taught through various cultural and social edicts that emotions were not to be expressed, which is completely inaccurate. Our emotions are in fact beneficial. They tell us about our subconscious programming, what is important to us, and what we need to do to restore safety to the nervous system. Decades of stuffed emotions had been liberated in the Vipassana experience, and it was time for me to pay attention.

Up to this point, I believed that I was "normal", and that trauma was something that only happened to war veterans. My Vipassana experience brought me to the undeniable conclusion that I had subconscious work to do. I did not yet know whether these were suppressed memories that I didn't want to deal with or if they were something else. Remarkably, I was no longer afraid of this process because Elaine Miller-Karas taught me that like any other injury, trauma can be healed.

CHAPTER 6

THE COMMUNITY RESILIENCY MODEL

Sincere thanks to Elaine Miller-Karas, MSW, LCSW and the thousands of CRM students, practitioners, and trainers healing the planet one nervous system at a time.

I was so impressed with Elaine's work that I became trained in the Community Resiliency Model (CRM)® and used these tools to deal with the overwhelming thoughts that were keeping me stuck in survival mode. The CRM tools offered a first glimmer of hope because Elaine taught me that what I was experiencing was completely physiological in nature. I wasn't crazy and more importantly I could learn to employ these tools to address my overwhelming feelings as they came into awareness via sensations in the body.

Elaine also taught me that there are specific signals that indicate when our nervous systems come back into balance such as: a deep sigh, shoulders relaxing, a yawn, a smile and tingling sensations in feet and hands. Therefore, it is equally important to notice sensations of a balanced nervous system, so that we can build awareness and find comfort in this experience. Miraculously, when we practice the CRM tools, we can actually widen our *zone of resilience*, the operating range of a balanced nervous system. As we practice, we build a greater capacity to deal with life's ups and downs.

Prior to learning the CRM tools, I believed that my fate was in the hands of a medical professional and the only way to lower stress was to take a drink or drug. I never for a moment imagined that I could proactively monitor and rebalance my own nervous system and through this process rewire a sense of well-being into my experience of life. Gaining this understanding marked another turning point in my life.

Here my friends was missing *puzzle piece number two*. I finally had some tools to work with the intense emotions that would arise both during meditation and in life. These methods worked for me! With continued practice, I no longer flew off the handle at the smallest inconvenience. I slept more regularly, and joy was slowly returning to my daily existence. I also became attuned to the sensations of well-being in the body and basked in the wonderful feeling of a balanced nervous system. For the first time in life, I enjoyed just being in my skin!

In the remainder of this chapter, I present to you these simple skills that changed my life. These skills are part of The Community Resiliency Model®, one of the many trainings offered through the Trauma Resource Institute in Claremont, California. I bow deeply and offer my sincere gratitude to Elaine Miller-Karas, MSW, LCSW and the many TRI practitioners who have shared these skills with the world.

To begin your journey, I invite you to find a quiet, comfortable place, free from distractions, and read through each of the instructions below. Give yourself ample time to absorb each practice. I recommend that you carefully read one skill at a time and take a few minutes to practice each skill before moving on to the next.

During the testing phase of this research, I discovered that some students prefer one skill over another. Given the different experiences that we encounter during the course of our lives, this should make perfect sense. Participants have also reported that different skills work best during different times of the day. So why not try each skill out for yourself and come to your own conclusions?

Resourcing: Our miraculous brains can do a lot, but multi-tasking is not one of these operations. We effectively process one experience at a time. We can use this processing limitation to our advantage. Whenever we notice that we are getting carried away by negative thoughts or sensations, we can consciously choose to place our attention on something else. It is helpful to choose something positive, or at least something that feels better than whatever we are focused on that is distressing to us.

Tracking: Many of us live "outside" of our bodies and instead spend endless hours in our heads, lost in thought. Tracking is a practice to gently get back in touch with our bodies via the sensations that arise as we place our attention on the body. Note, some sensations may seem overwhelming at first. Whenever this happens, you can back off that sensation by shifting your attention to another part of the body. Be patient with yourself and move at your own comfort. You are in charge of this experience. Also recall that you now have a tool to deal with intense sensations, which we learned in the preceding skill: resourcing. If you ever find that sensations in the body become overwhelming, you can return to your resource at any time.

Grounding: When we are lost in thought we can lose awareness of our environment. We can literally lose touch with our physical surroundings, as well as the sensations of the body making contact with the outside world. Grounding not only gets us back into the reality of our physical space but can also become an energetic way to interact through our bodies with the external environment.

THE "PRELIMINARY COMMUNITY RESILIENCY MODEL (CRM)® SKILLS:

Exercise: Resourcing

Bring to mind a person, place, thing, or idea that brings you great peace, comfort, joy . . .

Just thinking about this resource changes your mood and outlook on life.

Notice the sensations in your body: warm, excited, tingly, etc.

Notice as much as you can about this resource. If it is a place, what time of day is it? Is the sun shining? What are the smells in the air?

Intensify this experience in your mind and body and make it as real as possible as if you are with your resource right now.

Again, notice whatever sensations you are experiencing as you "live" this experience in the present moment.

Whenever you find yourself in an overwhelming situation, no matter where you are or who you are with, you can bring this resource to mind, placing your full attention on the experience of your resource.

Through a combination of breath counting and the consistent practice of CRM skills, I began to get comfortable with feeling the sensations in my body, as well as, the various sensations that accompanied arising emotions. Rather than stuffing them or running from them, I began to welcome these experiences. I discovered that it took a fraction of energy to let these emotions and sensations arise than it did to avoid them. Experiences of frustration and rage were slowly replaced with awareness and curiosity.

Before CRM, I was unaware of my nervous system, or state of regulation and dysregulation, and had no tools to rebalance. This kept me in a frustrated headspace. With a balanced nervous system, it was easier to find positive thoughts, and I was now able to spend greater amounts of time in positive mental states. A more consistently positive mental state allowed me to gain the ability to catch unhelpful patterns of thought and behavior as they bubbled to the surface. Wonderful! But with a greater awareness of my internal world, more questions arose. Why was I having so much difficulty with my emotions in the first place and why were these simple skills able to make such a powerful shift in my day-to-day experience?

During CRM training, I learned that during the first few months of development, a child does not have a fully functioning nervous system and must rely upon a caregiver for nervous system regulation. Having a mother with Bi-polar Disorder did not make for a stable environment, and I began to suspect that this parent/child co-regulation did not happen in my own development. I was becoming open to the possibility that I might have some degree of trauma to work with. I also came to believe that if I continued to practice the CRM skills, more information would emerge to direct my journey toward well-being. I was now ready to uncover the subconscious drivers of these intense emotions, through listening to the language of the body, sensations.

GOING DEEPER: SOMATIC EXPERIENCING THERAPY

I shared the extreme reaction that I had during the meditation retreat with my therapist. She recommended that I begin to work with a specialist in *Somatic Experiencing* (SE), a therapy that deals specifically with traumatic memories stored in the body. Missing *puzzle piece number three arrived.*

The SE therapist guided me back into childhood to explore what it was like growing up with a Bi-polar parent. As I began to talk about the most painful memories of my life, I felt the exact areas in my body where each memory was stored. Some memories were blocked for years, like the feelings of frozen terror in my throat as my mother screamed in my face, fists raised at the ready to strike, or the sadness in my stomach, when I was instructed to drag the Christmas Tree, lights, tinsel, and all, out to the bayou behind the house and throw it in.

Some memories were too painful to access or perhaps too early in childhood to recall. I could feel a sharp sensation in my body and sense there was a story there, but my brain would not or could not recall what had actually happened. The only thing I can liken it to is a blackout. Some events were just too horrific to remember and for those I would just stare at the floor and cry, knowing that in some way I was being protected from recalling that memory. It was a sort-of-necessary-amnesia that subconsciously sealed the past from conscious awareness.

The therapist explained that we needed to move slowly to give the body and mind time to gently experience and then release these intense sensations and subconscious memories. All the while the therapist continually reinforced that these experiences were in the past and that we were safe in the present. For years I rationalized that my brain was working independently of my body. But in fact, each mental, physical, and emotional event, from the womb up to the present moment, had been stored in the cells of my entire being, and were now manifesting in current life as habit patterns for survival.

After my third session the SE therapist diagnosed me with Post Traumatic Stress Disorder (PTSD). I had no idea that this was possible for someone like me. I had not served in the military, and I thought my upbringing, although abusive, was not traumatic. These SE sessions were mentally, physically, and emotionally draining, but afterwards the aches and pains in my body began to diminish. A lightness returned to these places in the body and after each session, I could breathe a little easier.

How could talking about past experiences relieve pain in the body? My friend, this is a field of study unto itself. But I will share with you three books that have been instrumental to healing:

Elaine Miller-Karas (2015). *Building Resilience to Trauma: The Trauma and Community Resiliency Models.*

Peter Levine (1997). *Waking the Tiger.*

Bessel van der Kolk (2015). *The Body Keeps the Score.*

CHAPTER 7

THE MESSENGER

I knew that my biological father was unfaithful to my mother and heard stories of how Marvin would go to work events and introduce another woman as his wife. These details would invariably make their way back to my mother, which must have been unbearable for an 18-year-old wife. As fate would have it, my dad returned to the scene around the time of my own emotional spelunking, anxious to reconnect with the child he had abandoned some 40 years prior. I held no animosity toward this human but felt no special bond as one might expect would occur between a long-lost father and child. No matter how much I pictured that Hollywood scene, the magical moment of father-daughter connection, the attachment was not there. I felt warmth toward Marvin, but nothing more.

Marvin did, however, share information that was challenging to hear, but extremely helpful in my quest for healing. He explained how while I was a few weeks old, lying in my crib, he witnessed my mother violently pound upon my chest during a fit of rage. Marvin pulled her off me. At which point she took a handful of pills in an attempt to end her own life. Marvin spent the night trying to keep his wife awake and alive. He saved both of our lives that night and for this I am grateful. Marvin said that he did not know why he needed to tell me this, but I sensed this was a terrible secret that he had carried for years, and his confession relieved some of the burden.

Enter *puzzle piece number four*: I had suffered what is known as *preverbal trauma*, or a life-threatening event that happens before the brain and nervous system can process memories. Childhood trauma rewires the brain and nervous system to function differently than non-traumatized children. I now had a name for the physiological consequences of this traumatic experience, *toxic childhood stress*. A condition in which the amygdala and hippocampus, networks in the brain involved in learning, memory, and emotional processing, are altered (Shonkoff, 2011). These are the same systems on which childhood development, behavior, and health depend. Through this traumatic experience as a newborn, I had developed a subconscious survival pattern that I was still relying upon as an adult. My mind had developed a story that allowed me to believe that everything was fine, but underneath this illusion, my body kept the score.

TRAUMA, THE FAMILY DISEASE

I had often wondered why my biological father left while I was still an infant. During one of his visits, Marvin recounted how, at the age of five, he was so hungry that he could not sleep. He lay awake all night trying to come up with a plan to feed himself. At first light he wandered the neighborhood and found a machine shop that was open. He went in and asked if he could sweep the floors to earn enough money to buy breakfast. And that day, at the tender age of five, Marvin became employed and found a way to survive, but the trauma of childhood poverty and neglect left a lasting impression on his young nervous system, which carried forward into the next generation.

Marvin was 70 years old when he told me this tragic story from his childhood, but the pain was as fresh in his mind as it was on the night of this indelible event. I came to understand that Marvin's abandonment of his own family was inevitable. He did not have the resilience to deal with a Bi-polar spouse and newborn child. He was simply doing the best he could with the limitations of his own nervous system.

Like so many of our ancestors before us, the cycle of neglect and abuse repeats generation after generation, without end. That is unless we each learn to utilize tools to stop this cycle of generational trauma. I now have a name for my condition, *Post Traumatic Stress* (PTS), and an explanation for why my nervous system often senses danger that is not there, necessitating behaviors that are inappropriate in the situation at hand. For example, a rustle in the bushes typically arouses a mild curiosity in my fellow hikers, while my nervous system has propelled me a foot into the air and off the trail.

You may be wondering why I shifted terminology from PTSD to PTS. *Post Traumatic Stress Disorder* is a clinical diagnosis. As Elaine taught, trauma is a wound, that can be healed. We are moving out of a diagnosis and into a course of action that will address and heal the condition of *Post Traumatic Stress*. That's a big difference!

COLLECTIVE TRAUMA

Let us pause for a moment and get honest about the state of the world in which we live. In the past decade, our planet has undergone extreme ecological and political changes, impacting our physical and mental health on a grand scale. This collective trauma has not yet been captured in scientific data, however the signs are everywhere as violence, suicide, drug abuse and child abuse are steadily rising.

More of us have experienced some type of mental, emotional, sexual, or physical abuse during childhood than we acknowledge as a society. This has a direct correlation with the decline in our mental, physical, and emotional well-being in adulthood. Awareness is the first step in stopping this cycle. The following is an inventory for each of us to assess how adversities experienced during childhood may have an influence on our adult lives.

EXERCISE: THE ADVERSE CHILDHOOD
EXPERIENCES (ACE) INVENTORY
(FELLITI ET AL., 1998)

This survey is a tool to identify potential challenges to well-being. How many of the following questions apply to you?

1. Did a parent or other adult in the household often or very often swear at you, insult you, put you down, or humiliate you? Or act in a way that made you afraid that you might be physically hurt?

Yes   No   If yes enter 1 _____

2. Did a parent or other adult in the household often or very often . . . Push, grab, slap, or throw something at you? Or ever hit you so hard that you had marks or were injured?

Yes   No   If yes enter 1 _____

3. Did an adult or person at least 5 years older than you ever touch or fondle you or have you touch their body in a sexual way? Or attempt or actually have oral, anal, or vaginal intercourse with you?

Yes   No   If yes enter 1 _____

4. Did you often or very often feel that no one in your family loved you or thought you were important or special? Or your family didn't look out for each other, feel close to each other, or support each other?

Yes   No   If yes enter 1 _____

5. Did you often or very often feel that you didn't have enough to eat, had to wear dirty clothes, and had no one to protect you? Or your parents were too drunk or high to take care of you or take you to the doctor if you needed it?

Yes   No   If yes enter 1 _____

6. Were your parents ever separated or divorced?

Yes   No   If yes enter 1 _____

7. Was your caregiver: Often or very often pushed, grabbed, slapped, or had something thrown at them? Or sometimes, often, or very often kicked, bitten, hit with a fist, or hit with something hard? Or ever repeatedly hit at least a few minutes or threatened with a gun or knife?

Yes   No   If yes enter 1 _____

8. Did you live with anyone who was a problem drinker or alcoholic or who used street drugs?

Yes   No   If yes enter 1 _____

9. Was a household member depressed or mentally ill, or did a household member attempt suicide?

Yes   No   If yes enter 1 _____

10. Did a household member go to prison?

Yes   No   If yes enter 1 _____

Now add up your "Yes" answers: _____This is your ACE Score.

According to this line of research an ACE score of four or more has a direct correlation to adverse health challenges. This means that not only does your risk of developing illnesses such as diabetes and cardiovascular disease increase, but also your risk of social challenges like maintaining healthy relationships or holding down a job. As one's number of ACEs increase above a score of four, so does the level of risk with each added ACE. Therefore, the higher the ACE score the greater the risk of mental and physical illness, addiction, incarceration, and suicide.

Does this mean that anyone with an ACE score of four or higher will experience mental, physical, or social challenges? Not at all! There are protective factors, such as having access to a loving caregiver, mentor, or social support network. And then there is just good old-fashioned variability. Some humans are blessed with an orientation to life that keeps them protected against illness no matter what is happening in their external environment. The important takeaway from the ACE study is that there is an undercurrent of abuse and trauma in modern society that is affecting our most vulnerable population, children who have no choice in the matter. This is a challenging fact to digest, but we can no longer turn a blind eye to this information. The question is now what can we do about it?

If you believe that trauma only happens to other people, then you may be burying reality under your own defense mechanisms. In children who have experienced a critical number of ACEs, Toxic Childhood Stress rewires the nervous system into a hypervigilant state wherein the child no longer feels safe (Shonkoff et al, 2014). Fortunately, there are steps that can be taken to address Toxic Childhood Stress, once again thanks to neuroplasticity, our brain's marvelous ability to wire new connections through new experiences.

As adults, we have the opportunity to break the cycle of generational trauma and learn more loving and trusting ways to interact with others and with our environments. That's a promise that we can count on. As we move through this book, we shall explore multiple avenues to create new experiences in the bodymind and in doing so, allow for greater opportunities to heal trauma.

Through self-study, I discovered my tendency to gravitate towards harmful situations. I also discovered that it is difficult to heal in the presence of toxic people and environments. Imagine if you can, that you are unconscious in a burning building. Fortunately, firefighters arrive, extract you and begin CPR to save your life. Now imagine that after being saved from a burning building you decide to run back into the burning building!

A warrior does not allow others to control, dominate, or harm them. Nor can we remain in an unsafe place for extended periods of time. We must forge a path away from toxic people, places, and situations. This is perhaps the most frightening part of our initial journey, to abandon the only way of life that we know. Take comfort in the fact that we have experienced hardships and survived. I love the story of the oyster and the pearl. The grit in an oyster's shell is required for formation of a pearl. Similarly, the grit in each of our lives is the basis for personal growth and evolution. While we may have wished for a storybook life, the grit is what makes us great! As a survivor you have the gift of grit. Now is the time to be patient with yourself and become willing to explore healthy scenarios that will facilitate healing.

CHAPTER 8

HEALING THROUGH RELATIONSHIPS

I now sit in awareness that everything I once believed to be true in my life was in fact a fabrication born out of trauma and protective patterns for survival. It was time to let go of the past and embrace the present. Once I became open to the infinite possibility of the present, the first in a line of life altering coincidences occurred.

Just a few short months after the proverbial bottom fell out of my life, I met a wonderful human in my graduate school program. She too was a seeker, healing from her own life challenges. I told her about my past and the work I was doing to heal myself. I expected the worst but instead received compassion. I told her about my family and history of addiction and mental illness, and she recommended a support group that might help me to address these wounds. Fortunately, she had the right message at the right time and helped me to find my way into a 12-step meeting.

TWELVE STEP SUPPORT GROUPS

The first meetings were torture. I felt that I did not belong there with these really screwed up people. Granted, it would be hard to get more screwed up than I was at that very moment, but this fact escaped me at the time. My chaotic mind was back in action, ready to run at the sight of danger, and then it happened, I heard another person telling my story in their own words; physical abuse, alcohol abuse, emotional neglect, and how the tools of this 12-step program made life manageable.

I needed all the help that I could get and so I kept going to meetings, found a sponsor, and worked the steps. Through this exploration I learned that my ego, which included all of the thoughts and perceptions about life, was fueling a good deal of the difficulties in my life. More importantly, the way forward was through letting go of the self-centered attitude that had been my primary defense mechanism over the years. I had never considered how my belief that the world was created to serve my needs before all others was the very mindset that kept me from opening my heart and healing family wounds. This was the turning point that set me on a new trajectory. It was now up to me to continually investigate my thought processes and to challenge the victimhood belief patterns that were in fact a barrier to my own growth.

The 12-steps complemented talk and somatic therapy and helped me dig deeper into the circumstances in my past that had led to the outmoded behaviors of my present. One of the big *a-ha!* moments was that when I was a child, I had no sense of safety. The unfortunate result was that I developed coping mechanisms that were all about trying to please the parent, caretaker, or significant other, often at the expense of my own safety. When these attempts to appease failed, my childhood strategy was to run away from the discomfort. I was still a runner through and through. I had a history of running from careers and even geographic locations. Let's put it this way, my grandmother kept my information in pencil in her address book.

I began to understand the detrimental impact that survival strategies learned from childhood had on my adult relationships. When we constantly try to guess what other people want or need and falsely believe that we are the ones that can give it to them, we set up a cycle of codependency in which no one comes out a winner.

I came to understand that each of us is responsible for creating our own sense of safety and for learning to regulate our own emotions. My emotions are my responsibility, and others' emotions are their responsibility. This simplifies life tremendously. Most importantly, I came to realize how codependency altered my perception of reality. I thought that I was a strong person who had it going on. It never occurred to me that I came across as a neurotic wreck.

It had taken me 45 years to develop the habit patterns that made me miserable. Real lasting change would take time, but I wanted fast, immediate relief—the quick fix without the side effects. I wanted to be a totally different person, living a totally wonderful life. These were expectations based upon fiction. Through introspection, I came to realize that I was still the same third grader looking to escape life rather than experience it fully. Furthermore, I came to understand that my perceptions were still those of a third grader in fear for her life. Better stated, my mind still had the same operating system for survival created under very different circumstances. My mind believed that the world was a minefield of disasters waiting to happen. I was not worthy of success; I would most likely fail at anything that I attempted because I believed that things just didn't work out for me.

THE VALUE OF FRIENDSHIP

As history came into focus, I felt as though the rug had been pulled from under my feet. Who was I without this storyline? In that moment of lostness, I had the good sense to reach out to my dear friend Zan. I met Zan when I moved from New York to Los Angeles some twenty years ago. She managed a quaint apartment complex of ten bungalows centered around a crystal blue swimming pool. We were fast friends who shared a fondness for spiritual seeking and adventure travel. Zan introduced me to sea kayaking and downhill skiing in the local SoCal mountains. Zan was the type of person that I could share a bottle of wine with and effortlessly kill five hours just hanging out and talking about the weather.

Over the years Zan had become one of my greatest cheerleaders in life, and after a quick phone call, she graciously decided to come out and check on me. She arrived at my monk like room in the Russian Village of Claremont, unfurled her sleeping bag, and we set off together for a hike in the Claremont Wilderness Area.

As we took in the fresh air and marveled at the rolling Chaparral, Zan reminded me of how successful I had been over the years, and how

I had excelled through each of my career choices. Zan also reminded me of how brave I was to leave a dysfunctional marriage and a corporate job, to take the time and opportunity to find myself and create a life that complemented my evolving world views. She then joyfully asked if I was seeing anyone special to which I retorted, *Yeah, right, the world is full of meditating, hiking, academics on a quest for spiritual fulfillment!*

After assuring Zan that I would be single for a very long time, she replied with a smile, "You never know who is around the next corner." Zan was the breath of fresh air that I needed to recall my depth of abilities and past successes. Sometimes a contrary opinion is exactly what we need to see the possibility in any challenge that we are facing.

The next week my new friend from the graduate program called and asked if I would like to join her for a morning meditation at the McAlister Center at the Claremont Colleges followed by a hike. Coincidence? Probably so. Off I went to a wonderful group meditation followed by a hike to Potato Mountain, well, more of a hill than a mountain, but our conversation was captivating.

I learned all about her upbringing, her research, and her burgeoning interest in Buddhism. The weather was perfect, the hike was exhilarating, and the day flowed effortlessly. I thought to myself that I had found a wonderful friend and was grateful for the opportunity to get to know her better. From the top of Potato Mountain, I gazed down at the City of Claremont and back at my new friend and then felt her hand reach for mine softly interweaving her fingers between mine. She then reached up and kissed me gently on my lips. All I could do was smile. This day was unfolding better than anything I could have conjured in my imagination. I stumbled for words and could only come up with, *Would you be willing to go out with me on a date?* To which she replied with a smile, "What do you think this is?"

So, life is wonderful right? Not by a long shot! I had just begun to work with the unprocessed trauma that permeated every aspect of my being. The first few weeks of our relationship were rife with misunderstandings and hurt feelings. I did not yet know how to navigate the discomfort of intimacy without running away. I also began to see that no human being on the planet can soothe my emotional pain. I began to rely instead upon an evolving *spiritual connection*, which I had culti-vated in the 12-step program. I also came to see this romantic partner as a magnificent teacher, exposing every insecurity and attachment chal-lenge that I carried from childhood into adulthood. I now had a choice, to learn from each unpleasant experience, or to continue operating with the old life plan of running from pain, burying my feelings, and worrying about all of the things in life that were out of my control.

Fortunately, my new love was on a similar journey of self-exploration and healing from her own relationship challenges. We were each explor-ing therapy for our own self development and mutually decided to begin couples therapy within the first few weeks of our relationship. Through willingness and mutual respect, we somehow endured the various trials and tribulations of the first months of a new relationship. But all was not well. So, we got married.

My partner had a temper. I noticed when we first started dating that seemingly insignificant actions like my eating pita chips before dinner would set her into a rage. Over the months she slowly became a more volatile person, flying off the handle at the smallest of infractions. As these emotional outbursts became more common, my nervous system began to react at a subconscious level, and I would drop into a *fawn* state. Recall that fawn is a lower energy state marked by attempts to seek safety through nurturing behaviors. I would touch her gently on the back and ask how I could help in the kitchen. As her anger escalated, I would withdraw emotionally unable to speak and unsure of what to say that would restore harmony.

How did this idyllic relationship turn intolerable? I did not yet un-derstand how we seek out the familiar in our relationships. If we grew up with an emotionally immature parent, we find this behavior familiar and perhaps even comforting in romantic partners. This is part of what I found attractive in my partner. Or so I thought. After a few months I could no longer endure the emotional tantrums.

The sensations in my body felt very similar to childhood, such as, clawing in my stomach, tightness in my throat, and throbbing in my head. Similarly, childhood feelings of helplessness began to emerge and again I found that I was trying to control an uncontrollable situation.

What I came to discover was that there was nothing I could say or do to change our interactions. I did not have the tools to help regulate her nervous system, nor did she. I slowly came to realize that this was no longer a safe or supportive relationship. I began to trace the events that led to yet another romantic nightmare and noticed a strikingly familiar pattern going all the way back to my first girlfriend in high school. What was driving these attractions that were destined to fail?

ATTACHMENT STYLES

A therapist once suggested that attachment style played a role in the dissolution of my first marriage. I was in enough pain to finally do some digging and try to sort out this attachment business. As luck would have it, George Haas, founder of *Mettagroup* in Los Angeles, was holding a meditation and attachment workshop the following weekend.

George's work combines Buddhist theory, Attachment Theory, and Vipassana meditation to help his clients address their attachment conditioning from childhood. In the second class of the workshop George described a classic interaction between two people with different attachment styles, which fit my current relationship to a tee. One partner desperately reaches out for soothing from the other, but the other is so overwhelmed with their own emotions that they cannot respond effectively. The demands grow, tensions grow, and over time, both partners become overwhelmed with the dissatisfaction of their unmet needs. As one therapist commented, "The bite fits the wound," or one partner's behaviors perfectly fit the dysfunction of the other partner's attachment style.

As my own relationship continued to deteriorate, I knew this to be true. While I sat on the couch desperately trying to connect with my partner, tears streaming down her face screaming to be understood, all I could do was sit quietly, frozen in anticipation of what might happen next. Our incompatibility intensified both our nervous systems' dysregulation. So it went, until we could no longer feel safe in each other's company. Another divorce.

Childhood trauma permeates many aspects of adult life and attachment style is yet another manifestation. My disorganized attachment style, resulting from childhood neglect and abuse, was very much a driver in the romantic partners that I selected. Until I began the work of repairing this attachment style, I was destined to repeat the same dysfunctional patterns and relationships over and over again. It was a painful lesson, but a relief to finally pinpoint the root cause of my relationship challenges and to have clear direction to create change.

AUTHENTICITY

Our interactions with other beings are yet another layer of the learning process that we can either choose to embrace or ignore. Many of us seek validation or a sense of identity through our relationships with others, however, we must first learn to be comfortable as our own unique and independent being. For those of us with chaotic childhoods this may present a challenge, for we believe that a sense of self and safety can only come through validation from another. This, of course, is a set up for disappointment because either we do not have a clear idea of what a healthy relationship looks like, or there is no possible way that another person can live up to our unrealistic expectations. This notion is also detrimental to our own development because in expecting another person to solve our problems, we give up our power to be who we truly are and to experience what we alone can accomplish through finding our authentic selves.

I have come to believe that life offers up the perfect lesson plan to help each of us evolve into something greater than our current selves. Regarding our choices in relationships, I recently heard a therapist describe it this way, "We marry our childhood problems." My hope is that this is not a requirement for adulthood, and perhaps with awareness we can learn how to stop repeating unhealthy childhood patterns before we marry our problems. Each new relationship is part of a unique lesson plan that presents a space to explore the type of person that we hope to become. I continue to explore this dynamic in my current relationships.

In the beginning of this journey, I wanted to run away from any discomfort that I felt. This was my only strategy for coping with difficult emotions. With an understanding of trauma, and a toolkit to deal with overwhelming emotions, I now have other options. Rather than run away, I choose to stay still, and become curious about the thoughts, emotions, and reactions that emerge during daily life.

Each of us is destined to repeat unexamined habit patterns. The alternative is to bring awareness to these patterns by watching them and learning from them, for we are not our emotions. We are in fact a witness to any experience happening within a limited field of awareness.

For example, certain thoughts of my second wife would trigger an explosion of pain in the center of my chest, tears would well up in my eyes, and a burning sensation would travel from my throat up to the soft palate of my mouth. When I calmly breathed through this experience and the accompanying sensations, I noticed how the burning begins with a great intensity then slowly subsides with time. Once I decided to let go of mentally analyzing the experience, I could begin to let these sensations arise, not trying to stuff them down, or change the intensity, but just let them do what they needed to do. Through this practice old memories and sensations had space to release. Without such awareness, another codependent relationship would have endured for months or possibly years beyond the lessons that were waiting to be learned.

Through this new process of balancing the nervous system whenever challenging emotions arise and staying grounded in the present no matter what is happening, I could now sit with the intensity of an experience rather than run from the pain. By allowing myself to feel every ounce of an experience, I created bandwidth that allowed each moment to ebb and flow without restriction.

With time and patience, I could also notice the positive sensations and feelings of well-being that emerged after a releasing experience. It became evident that I had untapped potential to create my own healing. I had so many questions about this process that were beyond the realm of Western Psychology. I was eager to develop the wisdom needed to heal these deeper parts of myself.

Venerable Geshe Dorji Damdul and the author. Nalanda University
Historic Site, Bihar India.
Photo Credit: unknown

CHAPTER 9

PILGRIMAGE

I concluded that I had few tools to deal with the inevitable heartbreak that is part of being human. I needed a path of study to help me better weather the storms of life, to handle emotional pain, and to live more fully in the precious time that I still had left on this earth, and this was the short list!

LIFE IS NOT A PROBLEM TO BE SOLVED, BUT A SOLUTION AWAITING DISCOVERY

To find a solution to any challenge, we must first seek to understand its cause. As a researcher, I began to question the exact nature of the pain I was experiencing, so I could move beyond masking the symptoms and toward healing the root cause. For this, I would need to seek instruction beyond Western medicine. Once I had set this intention another coincidence occurred, a fellow researcher invited me to join her on a trip to study the teachings of Shakyamuni Buddha, in his native lands of Nepal and India. This spiritual pilgrimage was organized by students of B. Alan Wallace.

Wallace-la, as he came to be known, is an esteemed researcher, as well as, a former monk and student of His Holiness the 14th Dalai Lama. He advocates the use of introspection to investigate the intersection between science, philosophy, and contemplative practice. Wallace-la has organized a team of researchers and students to empirically test many of the tenets of Tibetan Buddhism. Some of the questions under examination at the Center for Contemplative Research:

> Can Westerners develop attention to the point that they can experience greater introspection and clarity?

> Can Westerners understand the fleeting nature of hedonic pleasure such as material possessions and pleasant experiences?

> Can humans cultivate genuine happiness, a type of happiness that does not require external conditions?

It was during this trip to India that I met Venerable Geshe Dorji Damdul, director of Tibet House India. When we exited the bus in Sarnath, the site of the very first teaching the enlightened Buddha gave on the Four Noble Truths, there stood Geshe-la (Geh-sheh-lah), smiling from ear to ear as he watched our group of jet lagged pilgrims exit the bus. Geshe-la wore traditional Tibetan monk's robes of maroon and gold, and brown socks and loafers, accented by a bright gold cloth bag slung across his right shoulder.

The group scurried toward the bus depot where the toilets and water fountains awaited. But I shot straight over to Geshe-la. He smiled and offered me the bottle of water that he had been given moments earlier by the bus driver. I declined out of politeness, but he insisted, so I took the water and took a sip, which seemed to give him great satisfaction. He gave me a look you might see on your mother's face after she feeds you a hearty meal. I too experienced a similar feeling upon seeing Geshe-la standing alone outside the bus depot. It was as if a long-lost uncle had returned with gifts to distribute to eagerly awaiting children. I'm not sure what we talked about for the 15 or so minutes in which the rest of the group were enjoying the comforts of the bus depot, but we were suddenly waved onto the bus once everyone else was loaded and ready to commence our travels for the day.

On the bus, Geshe-la gave a *Dharma* teaching, the teachings of the Buddha, on the *Four Noble Truths that explain the philosophy, practice and goal of Buddhism.* Buddha's *First Noble Truth* is that life can appear to us as constant suffering. We have all experienced varying degrees of pain, but suffering is what follows the pain. For instance, recall a time when your heart was broken. The moment our beloved leaves creates an event that we label as painful, but it is continuous *rumination* or thinking about this separation that creates suffering.

The *Second Noble Truth* is that we experience suffering due to our ignorance of the nature of reality. We mistakenly believe that we are a solid and unchanging entity, separate and independent from the rest of the world. We fail to recognize that we change every second of every day. We also get frustrated when things change on us!

The *Third Noble Truth* states there is a way out. For example, what if instead of having the belief that no one should ever leave us, we begin to accept that life is full of unexpected events? With this correct understanding of reality, we can experience life without trying to hide from or minimize the inevitable shifts that occur over a lifetime that are not in accordance with our likes and preferences. This may seem like a tall order to undertake on our own, which is why the Buddha offered a set of instructions.

The *Fourth Noble Truth* is that there is a path to end suffering; a roadmap of trainings to achieve liberation.

Our group toured many of the places where Shakyamuni Buddha had ventured some 2600 years ago, to share his teachings on methods for well-being. There was Rajghir, the site of Buddha's second teaching on the impermanent nature of life. This aspect of Buddha's teaching flows directly from the Four Noble Truths. People come and people go, and one day we too will flow away from another place, person, job, and eventually this body that we currently occupy. Everything is impermanent, even the planet that we occupy will one day be consumed by the Sun!

Some of the darkest days of my own life were the result of an inability to accept change. I can become so identified with a romantic partner or a certain career that when these situations change, I am devastated. The Buddha taught that if we can remain mindful of the *Truth of Impermanence*, and come to expect impermanence, rather than fear it, we will experience greater serenity in daily life.

As the bus pulled into the parking lot of this historic site, a flood of vendors selling trinkets and mementos from the local village surrounded us. One man had a blanket, which he laid out at the front of the bus and then produced a Cobra from a straw basket. I was not interested in being in the same area as a deadly snake, but as I watched from the window, I could not help but empathize with this beautiful, fragile being. The snake handler would push and prod the neck of the Cobra until it would flare the diamond adorned hood around his head. It was a magnificent sight, yet it was somehow very sad to watch this beast perform against its will. I wondered if the Cobra suffered, or if he just accepted that this was life, performing on a blanket in a parking lot under a cloud of diesel smoke?

Our bus lumbered out of the parking lot, and we traveled kidney punishing roads from one amazing ancient site to another beautiful and wondrous place of antiquity and significance in Buddhist history. Each place that we visited was accentuated by a talk by either Wallace-la or Geshe-la. I couldn't have asked for a more magnificent context, nor guides for an introduction to the teachings of the Buddha.

We traveled for many days immersed in the vast diversity of Indian culture. The magnificent food, the beautiful textiles, and yes even the afflictive parasites that preyed readily upon my uninitiated Western digestive tract. I along with one other pilgrim experienced the *dreaded two-headed monster* of vomiting and diarrhea that left me confined to the bathroom and living quarters of my flat in Delhi, for days. Here was a firsthand lesson in suffering and impermanence!

All the while I remained open to these truly remarkable conditions to not only hear the teachings of the Buddha, but to experience the uncertainty of the way in which each new day might unfold.

I had never been to India, but it often seemed as if I had spent many years in the company of Wallace-la and Gesha-la. This uncanny familiarity did not end there. Our group was visiting the Mahabodhi Temple at Bodhgaya, an ornately decorated stone temple adorned by hundreds of stone carvings of various *Buddhas*, enlightened beings, throughout history. Each Buddha was uniquely carved, some wore different robes, or sat upon different bases, such as lotus or wild beasts, or held a variety of mudras and ritual objects to signify the special teachings that each Buddha embodied.

The temple is surrounded by a series of stone walls, iron gates, and security checkpoints. Armed guards met us at the front entrance and each of us passed through a metal detector and bag check before proceeding to the next gate. These procedures and safeguards are unfortunately necessary due to threats by those who wish to cause harm to the visitors and structures on this site. It is an ordinary garden where a man sat in meditation determined to seek the causes and conditions of well-being. How can simple ideas for living prove so powerful for some and so threatening for others?

The inner garden surrounding the temple and Bodhi Tree, under which Shakyamuni became enlightened, was packed with monks, tourists, meditators, vendors, and a pack or two of wild dogs. The dogs were larger breeds, in the 30–50-pound range, well fed, and free of mange and disease, unlike the roving packs of dogs outside of the temple wall. The Bodhi Tree was adorned with brightly colored textiles, and a constant flow of visitors moving in queues toward the tree to touch their hands and foreheads upon the bark. The air was thick with sandalwood incense and a cacophony of chanting in myriad languages.

I noticed a man weaving through the crowd who walked right up to me, as if we had known each other for years. He was a Western man, dressed in monk's robes, who asked "Is that Alan Wallace?" I exclaimed, *Yes, it is!* "Well, this is auspicious"! He replied and then turned and walked toward the front of the group to get a better listen of the Dharma talk given by Wallace-la on the practice of Shamatha as a path to enlightenment. I don't know why this monk felt comfortable approaching me out of the hundreds of people in the area, but I began to suspect that I either had met him in some other circumstance or had known him before, perhaps in another lifetime.

Yet more unexplained events were on the way. One was the remarkable experience of our visit to the Buddha statue in the Mahabodhi Temple. Our group filed into the temple and I was immediately struck by a presence. The Buddha seated above us was a life-size golden statue with piercing blue eyes. It looked down upon us with a gentle gaze. As I looked into his eyes, I felt a warmth in my chest that radiated down both arms and filled my body with heat—so much heat, in fact, that I had to peel off my jacket. The jewels surrounding the Buddha's head shimmered like mirrors on a disco ball, sending shards of light in every direction. I was speechless, tears rolled down my cheeks, and I had a great sense of longing. I'm still not sure what was happening within this remarkable place during this exact moment but for me this experience was powerful! I had come to India to explore how to deal with the challenges of life and my inner world was beginning to shift, as was my concept of reality. What is this experience we call life? Was I perceiving it accurately?

Over the course of several days, it slowly dawned upon me that I was asking the wrong question. Rather than wanting instructions on how to deal with the disappointments in life, I was more interested in discovering how to BE happy.

In the West we are taught from an early age that if we make enough money, we will be happy and safe from hardship. Yet no amount of money will prevent life from taking a challenging turn, a relationship from ending, or the inevitable experience of our own sickness, aging, and death.

Wallace-la introduced me to the concept that each of us has a natural happiness that resides within. He suggested that the teachings of the Buddha can enable us to uncover this natural, genuine happiness. I was thrilled to learn that happiness is our natural state and that suffering, although part of life, need not be the focus of our existence.

HAPPINESS 101

Geshe-la and Wallace-la helped re-orient me toward happiness and exploration of the causes and conditions of happiness. It turns out that many of us have the whole concept of life a little backwards. We seek to be happy at all costs and thus avoid what life *is*, a roller coaster of experiences and emotions; that is sometimes wonderful and sometimes damn painful. This is the basis of the Buddha's teachings. He specifically pointed out that our *desires* are a setup for suffering. We are worried that we won't get what we want and when we get what we want, we fear that we will lose it. Or, as my grandmother frequently lamented, "You're damned if you do, and damned if you don't."

Many of us also live under the illusion that our world was created for human comfort. The very conveniences that we have created to live more comfortably are the conditions for yet another form of suffering. We crave what we don't have, while ignoring all that we do have.

Geshe-la blamed our confusion upon one shared human challenge; we are ignorant of how interconnected we all are. This is particularly true in the United States where we emphasize individuality. We fail to comprehend how the natural resources that our planet provides are materials to manufacture the things we need, and we do this through cooperative work. For example, asphalt is manufactured from aggregate and bitumen and used to build roads that enable trucks and truck drivers to transport—in a supply chain—soil, water, and seeds, that farmers use to create the food that sustains life on this planet. This is but one example of all the human cooperation and natural resources that come together to facilitate our daily existence!

Another beloved teacher that you may be familiar with is Thích Nhất Hạnh, Thiền Buddhist monk and author, who refers to this co-creation of the conditions that sustain life as *interbeing,* because we all exist in relationship to all other beings on this planet whether we have come to this realization or not.

The outcome is that many of us suffer from a self-centered attitude that causes us to strive for our own comfort and safety without concern for others. Unfortunately, this is the very belief that closes our hearts to the possibility of connection with others, as we fold inward into a protective state. Many of us can take this experience into the extreme belief that the world is "Out to get us." This fuels the delusion that we are alone and isolated in our experience of life.

With a little introspection, we might notice how a self-centered attitude is not only harmful to those around us, but also to ourselves. This orientation toward seeking comfort at all costs pushes us towards things that help us escape what is going on within our bodies and minds. We have forgotten that the point of life is to be present with whatever is happening and not to get stuck in any single event because in reality conditions are ever changing.

We need to develop the skill of *bodhichitta,* or awakening heart, a method that allows us to be present for all of life's experiences, with a willingness to experience what *is*, rather than numbing or running from what we don't want to happen.

One of the students in our travel group asked why the Buddha taught meditation. Gesha-la suggested that we cannot correct what we are unaware of. The Tibetan word for *meditation* is *gom*. It means becoming aware of our minds and myriad conscious and subconscious thought patterns. To do so, we must assume the role of observer and watch whatever the mind is up to. As I have pointed out in several places in this book, this is one of the major objectives of meditation. Gesha-la also pointed out that it is not enough to simply watch our thought process. We must also actively replace negative thoughts with virtuous thoughts. Yes friends, the historical Buddha taught the modern concept of neuro-plasticity, wiring in the positive, thought by thought!

If Shakyamuni Buddha were alive today, he might be classified as a philosopher, psychologist, neuroscientist or physicist. But one thing is certain, the Buddha was a researcher first and foremost and teacher second. As with any good researcher, his theories are open to investigation. The Buddha asked that no one take his methods on sheer faith, but that each of us must put these practices to the test in our own life experiences to determine if they are of value. This is what I set out to do. I returned to the United States determined to continue this precious education.

Shifu, Taiwan.
Photo Credit: R.K. Rodgers

CHAPTER 10

BUDDHISM

Buddhism is not a religion, it's a practice, similarly to yoga, which you can do irrespective of religious beliefs – Thích Nhất Hạnh

I did a quick search for Buddhist temples on the Internet and found a monastery located less than five miles from my apartment, a short 15-minute drive by scooter. I was a PhD student, did not have a job, and my academic research, which consisted of exploring the various schools of thought on causes and remedies of stress, consumed eight to ten hours a day. I spent the remaining hours hiking the Claremont Wilderness Loop and practicing meditation. It was the perfect scenario for intensive self-study and transformation.

On my very first trip to the monastery, I felt a sense of danger as I transitioned from the majestic Oak Tree lined streets of Claremont to the economically distressed area of Pomona in which the monastery was nestled. The road to the monastery was a jumble of discount stores, fast-food establishments and the occasional homeless soul pushing all their worldly goods down the street in a shopping cart. I admit that I had doubts about this adventure. As smells of fried chicken and sidewalk urine wafted across the street and hit me square in the face, I considered turning around and puttering back to the safety of the known, but the landscape shifted from the busy commercial area into a row of 1950's stucco homes with parched brown lawns. As I continued down the avenue, I almost overshot the black wrought iron gate that demarcated the monastery from its surrounding neighbors. The intercom box was a slight tip off that this was a gateway to something unusual within the neighborhood. Again, I felt trepidation. Why the intercom? Who would answer the intercom? Would I need to answer a string of questions to be deemed worthy to enter these gates? I buzzed, and a few moments later, a woman's voice energetically answered back, "Amituofo!"

I froze, my mind searching for the appropriate response to whatever this meant. *Um, I am here for the meditation class. This is um, Rhonda.*

"Of course! Come in, come in!" There was a buzz followed by the hum of the motors retracting the heavy gates into their open position. I now saw a pretty, yet simple church some 50 yards to my right and a row of three pretty, yet simple houses some 75 yards straight ahead. I slowly advanced my scooter, again with trepidation, not knowing what to expect.

A small figure exited the church wearing something similar to what I recalled from the "Kung Fu" television series of my childhood: brown robes, baggy brown pants, brown cloth slippers, and a shaved head. I had no idea if this was the female who buzzed me in or another perhaps male person. I had a brief recollection of how as a child I desperately wanted to be like David Carradine's character in the "Kung Fu" TV series. He was a master of Kung Fu who exhibited supernatural calmness in the face of danger. Would I too get a cool name, like Grasshopper or maybe Firefly? The androgynous figure watched me park my scooter and pull off my helmet. They then motioned with a hand to come this way.

The exterior of the church was guarded by a pair of 10-foot-tall Foo Dogs. This was my first tip off that this may have once been a church, but not anymore. For me, that was a good thing. I can't say that my experience with church or church-going people in the South was a positive one. Suddenly, I was feeling more excitement than trepidation. This tiny figure of a human, who may, or may not someday call me Firefly, was smiling and motioning me into this church-like establishment, dispelled all notions in my head that this was a dangerous place inhabited by negative humans.

As I approached this being, a woman's voice again said, "Amituofo!" followed by, "welcome Rhonda!" I could now see the feminine features of an Asian woman in her early thirties smiling ear to ear, waving to me from between the Foo Dogs, and moving us both into the lobby of the "not a church" main building.

I entered the glass doors and again found something very different from a church, a line of three other nuns exclaiming, "Amituofo!" and smiling ear to ear. I can't say that I have ever seen people with a genuine smile within the walls of a church. Perhaps this was just my perception of church. Either way, I was excited to be welcomed in such a pleasant way.

Another major difference between a church and this "not a church" was the vibe in this place. It was an enclave of tranquility. An array of skylights filtered natural light into every corner of the main entrance. Statues of Buddhas and Bodhisattvas lined both walls of the entrance, and a faint smell of sandalwood incense permeated every space in the building, as did the serenity of the nuns. I noticed that the nun who ushered me into the lobby had three black dots on the top of her shaved head. Again, I was transported back to the "Kung Fu" series, wherein David Carradine's character, Grasshopper, was tattooed with dragons once he became an accomplished Shaolin master. Oh man, this was getting good!

There were four other nuns in the building, each with the same traditional robes, shaved heads, and three black dots. A million questions popped into my head at which point a Western woman came over and introduced herself, "I'm Dara and I will show you around." Dara was born in California and had been coming to the monastery for five years. She wore a comfortable looking gray suit made up of a spacious cotton tunic and oversized gray cotton pants, accented by an embroidered patch of a hand holding a yellow flower. I wanted one of these!

Dara walked me into the dining hall and introduced me to another 10 or so *lay people,* those who came to learn Buddhism from the nuns. The mix was about fifty percent Asian Nationals who had been raised as Buddhists and fifty percent Westerners who were raised in other faiths and wisdom traditions, but found that Buddhism better suited their mental, emotional, and spiritual development. I soon discovered that this was the commonality that joined all of us in our attraction to the monastery. We came seeking solutions to live a more contented life and were willing to try something completely different to find it. Yes, these were fellow warriors.

I soon came to learn that this "not a church", was in fact The Middleland Monastery, home to nuns trained in the Chan lineage of Buddha's teachings. As monastics, the nuns have shaved heads and wear traditional brown robes and brown cotton slippers, accented by a knitted brown scarf and beanie when the temperature drops. The three black dots on their heads, *Jeiba*, are actually burn scars, given during one's precept ceremony as a monastic. The three dots symbolize a commitment to the Buddha, Dharma, and Sangha. The nuns take a vow to uphold the teachings of the *Buddha, or Dharma*, through devoting their lives to the *Sangha*, the community of both monastics, and lay people, seekers like me.

The nuns are Taiwanese Nationals trained in Buddhism at The Chung Tai Chan Monastery. Although Taiwanese is their native language, each of the nuns is proficient in English and have a brilliant grasp of the subtleties of Buddhist concepts that they gladly explain in English.

During my first visit I had one burning question. Finally, at the end of the evening, the Abbess, Venerable Jian Xiang Shifu, asked if we had any questions. Without hesitation, I raised my hand and asked what Buddhism was all about. I expected an hour-long sermon, filled with moral stories, and fables of monks and nuns in far-away lands, fighting unimaginable foes, but she replied with two words, "The mind." At that moment I felt as if I had come home. This simple statement made a tremendous amount of sense in a world that offered few solutions for living. However, as I drove back to Claremont in the chilly night air and saw my fellow humans scurrying from place to place, pushing shopping carts into the shadows, I seriously considered if I could go through with all this Buddhist stuff. It was all a bit much for a Westerner with no similar experiences to compare.

Fortunately, I decided to go back and not worry so much about the formalities but rather focus on the promise of training the mind. During my first few visits, I was overwhelmed with the peculiarities of the experience. Upon entrance into the monastery, I was instructed to bow to the Buddha statue in the hallway, remove my shoes and place them in the cabinet, slip on a pair of plastic sandals, and greet the nuns in the preferred, "Amituofo!" This indicated that I recognized the infinite potential, or Buddha nature, that resides within each of us. I would then store my belongings in the appropriate closet, walk to the Dharma Hall, remove my plastic sandals, enter the hall, and then perform three prostrations to the Buddha and Bodhisattvas at the main altar.

I was then instructed that the liturgy, the Heart Sutra, printed on a large, laminated card, was to be lifted to my forehead during a certain bell, and lowered to my chest at a certain bell, but never placed upon the floor, out of respect for the sacredness of the text. This is an excerpt from the *Heart Sutra*- a teaching transmission from Shakyamuni Buddha,

> Listen Śāriputra, form is emptiness and emptiness is form. Form
> is not other than emptiness and emptiness is not other than form.
> The same is true with feelings, perceptions, mental formations,
> and consciousness.

We would begin each class by reciting the Heart Sutra, which in my opinion was impossible to understand even though it was translated into English. The longer version of this text is a discourse between the Buddha, and another enlightened being who is describing the nature of reality, to yet another enlightened being. And this is the less confusing part of the exchange.

After singing the Heart Sutra, I and the other students would then sit in the Dharma Hall and receive instructions on how to meditate. We began with breath counting. What a relief! Finally, something that was familiar to me.

The instruction was simple enough; we were to use our breath as an anchor for the wandering mind. We were instructed to breathe in, then breathe out, and count "one." This instruction was repeated for each breath, in and out, then "two", in and out, then "three." When thoughts came up, which they always did, we were instructed to notice that our mind had wandered, and then gently return our attention to the breath and to begin counting again.

After breath counting, we would perform a walking meditation. The instructions were similarly simple, when walking, notice your heel touching the floor, your toe touching the floor, and keep your mind anchored on the process of walking.

One of the nuns would tap a wooden stick on the floor to get us started moving about the perimeter of the Dharma Hall at a slow pace. After a couple of minutes, she would tap the stick twice, indicating that we were to increase the speed of our walking. After a few minutes, three more taps, and again, we would increase speed, to the point where we were moving at a pace just shy of running.

Some students would move faster than others and the walking meditation soon took on the characteristics of a roller derby. Students would wait for a faster student to pass, then fall in line to pass slower students, all the while noticing the sensations of walking while not thinking about anything other than walking. And yes, you are correct, it is damn near impossible to be in a roller derby and not think about who you are going to pass, who is passing you, and whether your socks will slip out from under you if you go any faster.

Walking meditation practice helped me to maintain focus on the present moment once my body was in motion and other elements of existence entered this experience. It is far less challenging to maintain focus while sitting on a cushion counting one's breath, than to maintain a clear mind while weaving in and out of moving human bodies at a quickening pace. Both practices were beneficial for training the mind to be stable during the vicissitudes of daily life.

Once we made it through the Heart Sutra and sitting and walking meditation practice, we would adjourn to the Dining Hall for tea, cookies, and a *Dharma talk*, an explanation of how to translate the teachings of the Buddha into practices for daily life. In the first few weeks of rituals, meditation, and Dharma talks I felt nothing but chaos. My mind would spin about the formalities of the monastery, wondering whether or not I put my shoes in the right place, what in the world the Heart Sutra was talking about, and why meditate when all I could do was focus on the pain in my back and knees?

As time wore on, the rituals became second nature and presented a soothing method to shift from the mindset of the mundane, outside world, into the present moment tranquility of the monastery. I memorized the Heart Sutra and began to explore the meaning of the words.

Are the thoughts I am experiencing reality? Are the sensations in this body reality? If they are real, then why do these aspects of nature change so quickly and frequently? One day I am on top of the world and the next a sad mess. Which one is me?

The abbess's meditation instructions similarly evolved over time. Not in a linear way such that each session was better or worse than the next, but in a greater understanding that life ebbs and flows, as do our thoughts, the sensations in the body, and the body itself. Similarly, there was an evolution in my understanding of the Dharma teachings translated by the abbess. Little by little I could see how this information applied as a skillset in the outside world.

When I was a kid, I owned a Magic 8 Ball, a fluid filled globe with a small window in which one could peer and see different answers to life's big questions, "Should I pack my bags and join the circus?" The Magic 8 Ball would respond with, "Maybe." As an adult, I still had questions, such as how to feel about my existence in the world and how to respond to daily situations that overwhelmed my nervous system. The Dharma are a set of rules for life which instruct us how to respond to any situation for an optimal result, whether the challenge comes from situations in our external environment, or disruptions within our own bodymind.

I cannot say exactly when this combination of rituals, meditation, and Dharma teachings began to work their magic in my life, but little by little, I began to change. Day by day, the chaos in my mind diminished. The abbess would carefully answer each of my questions, not with opinions, but with the teachings of the Buddha. Life began to make sense to me. My understanding of my place within the world became less of a question and more of a practice. This practice gradually evolved into a calm, compassionate human engendering great care for not only humans, but all sentient beings on our planet.

I came to understand that the mind was malleable and that as thoughts changed, so did external circumstances. Life slowed down and it became easier to witness challenging thoughts and behaviors rather than getting swept away by them.

I now looked forward to entering the monastery, bowing to the Buddha in the hallway, swapping my shoes for the sandals, and making my way to the Dharma Hall for the nightly meditation and Dharma talk. Each meditation brought more peace to my body and mind. Each Dharma talk brought more clarity to the nature of my internal life, as well as my relationship with the external world.

For example, I once had a tremendous temper and believed that others were consciously choosing to disrupt my world. When someone cut me off in traffic, I honestly believed that they chose to cut me off, that I was the only person in this stream of thousands of cars that they picked for this offense, and that it was my responsibility to teach them a lesson. This is the epitome of a self-centered attitude.

The abbess reminded me of the principle of *causality*. Nothing in the world exists on its own accord; we live in an environment of cause and effect. There had been many occasions where I had cut others off in traffic. In fact, I once owned a fancy car capable of the most impressive maneuvers and used this to my advantage to weave in and out of traffic, sometimes at dangerous speeds. Somehow this fact escaped my attention while noticing what others were doing instead of focusing on my own behavior.

The abbess asked me point blank what I could do to improve my own thinking in this situation? I told her that I could remember all the times that I was guilty of this same self-centered behavior. I could have compassion for the driver that cut me off and open myself to the possibility that they were not thinking clearly in that moment. Or perhaps I had completely misread the situation, and they were rushing to an emergency. The abbess then asked me to notice how this change in perspective impacted me personally. Just by thinking about this situation from a different perspective my shoulders dropped, my heart rate slowed, and my body posture changed from folding inward to opening outward. Yes, through this simple act of changing my perspective on the situation, a transformation occurred within seconds in my physical body! This instantaneous change occurred without a drug, drink, or external distraction! This is but one example of the tremendous power of our minds.

WATERING SEEDS

Up to this point I had been using the Community Resiliency Model (CRM) tools to balance my nervous system AFTER something in the external world would trigger a response. But I was still trapped in a loop of reactivity.

Conflict is very uncomfortable for me. Whenever a person raises their voice or behaves aggressively in my presence, my heart would explode into rapid pumping, fight or flight survival mode. It would then take some time to realize that I was in an altered state and choose to employ the CRM tools to balance my nervous system. The CRM tools were highly effective in addressing the emotional nature of my reactions, but not the mental basis of these reactions. When I asked the abbess for a solution, she used the analogy of watering seeds in a garden. Our minds are the fertile ground, and our thoughts are the seeds.

The question then becomes, which seeds are we watering through our attention? Each of us has many different types of seeds planted within our minds: love, compassion, anger, fear, jealousy, and so on. Mindless repetition of the same thoughts keeps us trapped in a cycle of similar behaviors. What types of thoughts you may ask? Thoughts like the world is a dangerous place, people are unhinged, bad things happen every day. The realist in the bunch may counter that there is truth in these statements, but the flip side is equally true. Millions of people make it through each day safely surrounded by stable, caring humans unfettered by what might go wrong. A theme that we will revisit over and over in this book is that thoughts are malleable, and if we regard them as such, we are responsible for our mental creations.

You may be familiar with the definition of *insanity* as doing the same thing and expecting different results. As the abbess would point out during each of our conversations, "Keep doing the same thing if you are happy with the results." If I wanted to break my cycle of insanity, then I must first begin to water different seeds in my mind.

The abbess was skillfully explaining the basis of neuroplasticity, the ability to create new connections in the brain as we think new thoughts and practice new behaviors. I now understood that my thoughts had to change to diminish the spark of reactivity that led to reactive behaviors.

PRACTICE PAUSE: REDIRECTING PRACTICE

Can you be angry and joyful at the same time? Neither can I! We can use this biological fact to our advantage by working to catch our mind whenever it is going down a negative path. The sooner we catch ourselves thinking in a negative way, the better. The longer we spend on a negative thought, the more likely it will cascade into a thought spiral.

As we will learn, the more we think about something, the stronger that pathway becomes in our brain. For the next 5 minutes, I invite you to:

Watch the quality of your thoughts and notice when a negative thought arises.

Choose a more positive thought.

Repeat this process over and over.

Feel free to journal about this experience and note anything that might help you to understand your own behaviors and what you hope to change going forward. I invite you to revisit this practice whenever you find yourself moving toward a negative thought spiral.

Buddhism is both a path for exploring the contents of our minds, and a system to lessen the suffering that we create through our own thoughts and habit patterns.

CHANGE FROM THE INSIDE OUT

Let's take a quick peek under the hood to see what neurological changes were occurring during my time at the monastery. My thoughts were evolving through the practice of watering beneficial seeds in the mind to the point where I spent much less time in catastrophic thinking. I chose instead to place attention on all the good in my life and to practice compassion for others. The circuits in my brain were shape-shifting from old destructive thoughts and habit patterns to new beneficial ones. You might be wondering how long this will take. Diligence of practice can rewire a new habit within a few weeks. However, deeper patterns may take several months to years to rewire.

Meditation was also working to activate different circuits within the brain. It was reducing activity in the limbic system, my emotional responses, and shrinking the amygdala, my threat center, while strengthening connectivity to the prefrontal cortex, allowing me greater access to calm rational decision making (Hölzel et al, 2010).

But my meditation practice would often be interrupted by a barrage of sensations that we refer to as physical pain. During breath counting meditation I would count, "One," and all my attention would be drawn toward the pain in my right knee. My mind would then race for solutions to minimize the pain. *Should I get up? Change the cross of my legs? Sit through the pain and hope it will go away?* In short order, the endless stream of past and future thoughts would begin to roll a conversation, a scene from a movie, a memory from childhood, and on and on. Why was it so difficult to get past the discomfort in my body during meditation practice? Why would my mind begin to race at the first sign of pain?

PAIN AND ATTENTION

Physical pain is part of the bodymind's strategy for survival. When pain is present it is natural to invest all our resources into doing something to lessen it. But what is the connection between thoughts, sensations, and pain? If you've ever heard the phrase that pain "is all in your head," then you have part of the story (Moseley, 2004). For there are indeed *nociceptors,* specialized neurons in the body, that alert the mind when pain is present. But *pain,* signals that alert us of potential damage or injury, are interpreted by a sensorial system of present moment stimuli mixed with past experiences, or memories, of pain. These memories help us to determine the best course of action based on what has worked in the past to lessen the pain.

Through trial and error, we discover many ways to manage pain. For example, *diversion* is a strategy of finding something more "important" to place our attention upon, like shopping, a romantic partner, a movie, an all-consuming pursuit, or a steady stream of thoughts that I call "the jumble." These thoughts can range from deciding that I'm hungry to re-running a scenario from work that happened years ago. There is also the strategy of numbing the pain through medication, drugs, alcohol, or other substances that lessen the intensity of the pain signal to the brain. There are inherent perils within this strategy. Our tolerance shifts and over time we require greater doses of the substance to achieve the same relief.

Then there is the king of all pain, emotions! A cut on the hand will throb for a few moments until we apply cream and a band-aid and, voila, the pain lessens. Emotional pain goes on and on and on, unless we understand the nature of this system. Like physical pain emotional pain is a signal that we are in danger, but the strategies to lessen the danger are more elaborate. With the cut, we know intuitively to avoid the sharpness of the surface that produced the cut. With the death of a loved one, for example, we must endure the loss day by day to process the emotions surrounding this experience. This is where many of us fail to recognize the importance of our thoughts in the process of healing.

A student was grappling with emotional pain and the Buddha asked, "Is it painful to be shot by an arrow?" The student agreed that it is indeed painful to be shot by an arrow. The Buddha then asked, "Would it be even more painful to be shot by a second arrow?" The student again agreed. The Buddha then pointed out that the second arrow is the bodymind's reaction to the first arrow.

What can we do with this information? We can continue to avoid the feedback loop of pain. We can leave it unresolved in the bodymind, or we can address the second arrow and become an observer of the sensations in the body and thus create an opportunity to change our interpretation of the pain. This is where the philosophy of yoga sparked the next phase in my journey.

Bhakti Fest, Joshua Tree, CA. Photo Credit: unknown

CHAPTER 11

YOGA

Yoga is union of body with the mind and the mind with the soul.

—*BKS Iyengar*

As mentioned earlier in this book, synchronicities abound and when followed they can yield extraordinary benefits. One such synchronicity occurred when I joined a local gym to combat the stress of grad school. I would go in occasionally and work myself into a lather running as fast as I could on the treadmill, followed by a few rounds of weights, and then a collapse in the sauna afterward. This formula worked great for an hour or two after I left the gym. But the stress of life was back with me by bedtime.

One morning I entered the gym, greeted by the familiar scent of rubber bathed in copious amounts of antimicrobial disinfectant, scanning the room for a new cardio machine to distract me for 45 minutes. I noticed a group of jovial, tanned ladies clustered around a doorway to one of the group workout studios. Their demeanor struck me as different. The typical gym patron rushed from machine to machine barely making eye contact with others. These ladies were chatting, smiling, and relaxed. I was intrigued and joined the line.

The instructor was a smiling gentleman who opened the door and waved us in with pleasantries saying, "Welcome, good to see you all. We will begin in a seated position." This was a yoga class, and I did not have a yoga mat in my possession or have the slightest idea of what to do with one. The instructor noticed my uneasiness, smiled, walked over with a mat, and welcomed me to the class. We began by breathing. What a concept! I sat there crossed legged, focusing on the breath, and noticed the same pattern begin to arise as in my meditation practice. The first breath was no problem, but then a pain would come into my awareness, and my attention would fixate on the pain. My breath would shift from full, robust, and purposeful to shallow and withdrawn as my attention fixated on ways to mitigate the pain.

The instructor noticed my discomfort and recommended that I change the orientation of my legs, placing the soles of my feet together, and then moving my feet further from my body. This helped! I was able to breathe more comfortably and in doing so had a greater ability to hold attention on the breath. We then moved through a series of poses from this seated position. Some were movements of the neck, some movements in the spine, and some in the torso and legs. Each new pose was preceded with an instruction to breathe in with a certain movement and breath out with a different movement. Yes, we were still doing a breathing meditation, which was now coupled with a body movement. This was a full body awareness meditation!

The instructor then shared a most impactful suggestion, "Only move your body to the point where you feel a slight amount of resistance and then stop, go no further. Stay on this edge, breathe, and allow the tension in the body to release naturally." In this moment a change in perception occurred. I finally ceased pushing beyond my own comfort level and experienced firsthand the benefits of a slow release of resistance in the body. I could finally take a break from myself, my demands, my expectations, and my perceptions of what I should be capable of, like getting into advanced positions after only one yoga class. In this process, I was removing the second arrow from my meditation practice—me.

WHAT IS YOGA?

In the United States, the word, "Yoga" typically brings to mind the physical poses, or *asana*, as well as, a certain type of person, gender, or lifestyle. Admit it, many of you just flashed to spandex and Kombucha. *Asana* describes the mindbody practice that creates an awareness of the connection between breath, sensations in the body, and thoughts in the mind.

But what is yoga? It might surprise you to learn that many interpretations exist. One of my teachers taught that yoga is, "Pious and sacred and refers to a blissful state of the *soul* or innermost core of one's being" (Tandon, 2013). I love this definition for it goes right to the heart of the journey of yoga to establish a connection with that goodness, that Wallace-la and Geshe-la spoke of, that exists deep within our own souls. Other wonderful definitions of yoga include: a universal consciousness experienced in each cell of our bodies; a union of mind, body and spirit that recognizes the interconnectedness of the individual to the universal (Iyengar, 2005); and, perhaps the most practical definition of yoga comes from the "Bhagavad Gita," as *equanimity*, or being at peace within ourselves no matter what is happening in our internal or the external world.

SLOW MEDICINE

I wish I could tell you about how excited I was to continue this practice after the first class, but that would be a lie. I had little flexibility in body or mind. It appeared that the people around me could move effortlessly into the next asana while looking graceful and steady. This was the first challenge yoga brought to me; I had to learn to focus on my own progress rather than comparing myself to those around me.

I did continue to experiment and tried different types of yoga taught by different instructors. I noticed that each instructor would give directions on how to breathe and when to inhale and exhale with each movement. Apparently, this was an important detail.

In the beginning, breathing as instructed, with the appropriate movement was completely beyond my ability. My mind raced with endless thoughts ranging from self-criticism to judgments of others in the class, to what I was having for lunch, and the occasional punctuation of *boy this is painful!* and *I will never be any good at this*. I would notice a pain in my knee, put all my attention on this pain, and then realize that I was holding my breath. After a few moments I would remember to breathe and then have a distressing thought about a past event and then realize that I was holding my breath again. Fortunately, I did hear the instructor ask that we be patient with ourselves and trust that with continued practice, each one of us had the potential to progress on the path of yoga. Day after day, week after week, this is exactly what happened.

It may appear that yoga asana is all about the body but, in fact, it is a constant exploration of the connection between body, mind, and breath. Certain poses may appear beyond our ability, but as we patiently stretch the *fascia,* connective tissue within the body, we explore how to gently move into discomfort by utilizing the breath as a vehicle for release. What are we releasing?

This will differ from person to person. Sometimes it is just the tension of the day. For others it may be subconscious patterns of survival, such as the act of tensing muscles in anticipation of a harmful event. Similarly, we may subconsciously hold our breath in anticipation of potential disaster. Have you noticed how your breathing changes when you are about to have an unpleasant conversation or open a distressing email? Just as we build awareness of our subconscious thought processes through meditation, we build awareness of our subconscious somatic processes through yoga asana. Through this process of exploration, breathing, and releasing, we can begin to experience greater peace in the bodymind.

A PHILOSOPHY FOR LIVING

We previously explored how past experiences can be stored within the tissues of the bodymind. In yoga, the stored impressions of all intentions, thoughts, and actions that we have experienced during our lifetimes are known as *samskaras.* These experiences not only inform our understanding of the world but also contribute to the formation of behavior patterns. As a *yogini,* or researcher of the self, I can confirm that the majority of the negative habit patterns stored in my body were an attempt to escape mental and physical pain.

So how does yoga suggest that we work with our samskaras? The sage Patanjali stated, "Yogas chitta vritti nirodha." This roughly translates to yoga practice can quiet fluctuations of the mind. The deeper meaning is that yoga can be used to develop our ability to witness these fluctuations of the mind without getting carried away by them.

Similarly, we can work to free ourselves of the sensations that disturb us from the inside.

A memory may trigger a distressing sensation in the body. This is an opportunity to notice the sensation, feel the feeling, and let it go. Stuffing our feelings and sensations will only store this event to surface at a later time. If we allow the feeling to come up, witness it, allow it to be-as-it-is, and allow it to pass, this samskara will release naturally on its own. As we previously discussed, we begin this release by assuming the position of an observer, we watch our thoughts, watch the sensations in the body, and we do not identify with, or water, either of these transient phenomena. All that arises in the bodymind will release and pass if we allow it to do so. Yogas chitta vritti nirodha!

For those of us experiencing chronic stress, the wisdom tradition of yoga is a full course of therapy to gradually experience and then release these reactive patterns or samskaras stored in the bodymind. For readers in the West, you might be wondering how we can muscle our way through these changes or use willpower to move this process along quickly. In my experience, this process is the exact opposite of effort. I had to be willing to let go of any trying or "efforting" to be successful. In these moments of surrender, the bodymind did the releasing all on its own. Imagine that! We possess innate wisdom to heal ourselves and all we must do is get out of the way!

How can yoga work for those of us who have experienced trauma? Earlier, I touched upon the concept of living in a state of hypervigilance. For those of us who live in this space, our bodies and our minds are constantly oriented toward survival, which perpetuates rigidity in our physical body and limits access to mental flexibility. When we occupy this space life is a struggle, most of our energy goes toward survival. In the West, researchers have developed specific types of trauma-informed yoga practices, which are wonderful if you have access to this specialized training (e.g., Kabat-Zinn and van der Kolk). For millennia these same principles have been taught in the East through basic Hatha Yoga, physical movement combined with specific breathing patterns as a process to get our bodies back into sync, so living is no longer a struggle (Sadhguru, 2020).

Through the philosophy of yoga, we can learn to live in a position of comfort and ease by purposefully noticing our tendency toward rigidity and working toward suppleness in body and mind.

Some of you may have given yoga asana a try once and thought, "Not for me." Why is yoga so challenging? In my experience, I was accustomed to numbing or running from any type of discomfort. The challenge was therefore to develop an ability to experience yoga practices that brought up intense mental and physical discomfort, without running away. Asana practice teaches us to gently lean into the sensations of the body, not push too hard, not have any expectations, relax into the moment, and release stored tensions in the bodymind.

ATTENTION AND ASANA

Yoga asana are also opportunities to quiet the mind. At the beginning of each practice session, the yogi sets an intention for what we hope to accomplish. For me, the most important aspect of asana practice was safety. At each session, I would look at my yoga mat and consider it a *safe space* completely and utterly under my own control. I could work as intensely or as gently as needed on any given day, go into child's pose at any time, or curl into a ball and cry. This was my sacred space for discovery of the unknown, where I bravely went to experience anything that might come up. A space just for me, where I did not need to prove anything to anyone. This is the practice by which we slowly release samskaras, the perceptions stored in the bodymind, a little at a time.

It is important to note that asana are also a meditation practice, and another method to observe processes of the mind. Occasionally, my mind would protest as I leaned into discomfort. However, through honoring this edge, I developed a sense of mental safety as I allowed these sensations to arise through asana and then back off the pose whenever sensations became too intense.

Interestingly, similar to the Somatic Experiencing therapy (SE) I had done, certain poses brought up certain sensations and memories. Thoughts of Marvin, my biological father, were experienced in the stomach. Whereas thoughts of my mother were experienced in the throat. These stored memories were fleeting in nature just like the sensations in my body; I would breathe, watch them arise, and disappear.

Session by session the practice changed and so did I. Poses that were excruciating in the beginning were now part of my regular practice. Similarly, I viewed thoughts that would arise during asana as passing events; nothing to be grabbed onto or analyzed. This is the beauty of yoga, through slow, patient, practice we unravel the knots in the body and mind.

I became enchanted with yoga and decided to enroll in teacher training at a local studio in Claremont, California. I also found a nearby college that offered classes in yoga philosophy. I was ready to embrace this entire experience and to incorporate these principles into daily life.

I studied a particular style of yoga taught by BKS Iyengar that emphasizes working slowly and methodically to heal injuries in the body-mind. After a year of working with the breath and deepening my asana practice, I had a profound shift. The survival response that I experienced as a novice yogini that led me to leave practice whenever the sensations became too intense was now just another experience on the yoga mat. I now felt safe enough to explore these events, knowing that I could lean into or back away from each inner experience. The choice was mine. I brought this same orientation to meditation as well and decided that the meditation cushion would now be a safe space, where I could lean into or back away from any experience.

Lois, one of my early mentors, noticed this shift in my body and asked which particular asana I had been practicing to achieve it. I replied that nothing had changed in my asana, but as my mind had begun to relax so did my body. This is the magic of yoga. The body feeds information to the mind and the mind feeds information to the body, therefore, it makes perfect sense that ancient traditions that help us to gently reconnect body and mind through the breath, thoughts, and sensations, would aid in healing trauma.

I invite you to pay attention to the conversations happening between your own body and mind. Sometimes these may appear as a negotiation between the two and other times it might feel like a straight-out war, like my experience in Vipassana meditation. Once we embrace the wholeness of the bodymind we can listen in on the conversation and receive whatever message is coming forward. As we do so, we clear the way for deeper material to begin to surface. It is now time to work beneath the waves of emotion to uncover and deal with the root causes.

Mt. Baden-Powell. Angeles National Forest, CA. Photo credit: R. K. Rodgers

CHAPTER 12

WORKING WITH THE BODYMIND

When you begin to listen, you will discover a lot of nonsense coming from your own head.

—*R. K. Rodgers*

I have mentioned how both the body and the mind are a storehouse of all our previous life experiences. Each of us is operating from a set of programs that have been formatted since birth. For instance, if you had a parent or family member that showed an adequate degree of love and affection, you will most likely view the world as a loving place. If you lacked basic care as a child, then you may view the world as a dangerous, unloving place. Many of us grew up with a parent or caregiver that was incapable of creating a warm and supportive environment. Unfortunately, we may have internalized this person's behavior as part of our perceptual database. In Psychology we use the term *inner critic* for this malware in the perceptual database. For me, the inner critic is a little voice in my head that runs a loop of you're not good enough, not smart enough, not capable, and not worthy. Through constant tracking and checking in with the bodymind I have developed an awareness of moment-by-moment states in my body, and for me this inner critic has a definite posture: tense shoulders, shallow breathing, and a sense of dread that something bad is about to happen.

Awareness of one's inner critic is the first step to effectively dealing with this malware. When I notice a negative thought arising out of the blue, I check to see what the inner critic is up to. If the message is not kind or helpful, then I can be certain it is the inner critic.

The second step is to replace the unkind voice with a kinder alternative. For instance, I recently had a mouse in the ceiling of my home. The voice of the inner critic blasted a list of concerns: we don't want to harm the mouse, we can't get to this area without falling through the ceiling, you don't know how to handle this, what if the mouse invites his family and you get an infestation. I paused to see where this was coming from and noticed the tone of my parents' collective worry. I then replaced this critical narrative with, *I know how to do research! It's my vocational training, so yes, I can do this! I bet there are a thousand YouTube videos on this subject, and I have a group of friends I can ask about their own experiences, and for help in solving this problem.* Voila, the inner critic was shut down and replaced with a helpful voice, *I've got this*!

I have previously mentioned the power of positive thinking. Ponder this for a moment, everything that has ever been actualized into being on this planet began with a thought, from the Mars Curiosity Rover to what you made for dinner last night.[1] Our thoughts are the foundation of everything that we create. It is, therefore, important that we recognize the quality of our thoughts, including that inner critic, and that we take steps to redirect the negative and accentuate the positive in our thought stream.

We have now embarked on a critical part of our journey known as self-compassion. *Self-compassion* is often described as the act of being kind to ourselves. In Buddhism, self-compassion is treating ourselves with the same love and respect that we would extend to a dear friend or loved one. Therefore, letting the inner critic dominate our experience is not an act of self-compassion. If you are still convinced that this harsh voice is your friend, I now grant you the authority to banish it and thereby practice self-compassion every single day, from today until you draw your final breath!

You are now welcome to explore every aspect of your reality to

---

1. A shoutout to all my friends at JPL. Dare Mighty Things!!

not only find acts of unkindness, but also to eradicate them. Sometimes this means changing the internal narrative of our own unkind words, effectively replacing the inner critic with a kind friend or loving parent. Similarly, this means removing ourselves from unkind situations, or unkind relationships with others. Self-compassion is closely linked to *self-care*, which is the practice of tending to our mental, emotional, physical, and spiritual being to experience increasing levels of health and well-being. Dear friend, starting today, please give yourself the gifts of self-compassion and self-care. These are essential building blocks for the work that you are doing and are critical to progress on this healing journey.

As I began the new adventure of working with the bodymind I noticed that three practical things needed to happen each day for me to progress on the path of healing: breathing, moving, and trusting.

BREATHE

What was the first thing that you did when you entered this world? You took a breath. What will be the last thing that you do before you exit this world? You guessed it. The breath is a sacred connection to our own lives and what comes next, aka, the unknown. Isn't it amazing that you, I, and everyone that we know will stop breathing one day? Perhaps we should spend more time noticing this thing that ties us to our worldly presence.

We all know what happens when we breathe rapidly and shallowly, eventually we pass out! But many of us forget that we have control over a powerful internal regulator of our nervous systems, the breath. When we purposefully breathe deeply and slowly, we bring more oxygen into the lungs and body. This feels good! With each exhalation we engage the calming part of our nervous system which physiologically improves how we feel in that moment, but there is another powerful aspect of internal regulation tied to the breath, our attention.

It is easy for human attention to focus on some unhealthy places. For many of us with *anxiety*, we have built our lives around imagining all that could possibly go wrong. I have found that anxiety results from believing that I have control over some outcome that is completely beyond my human abilities. My attention is then sucked into running myriad scenarios none of which will ensure that the outcome I desire will manifest. This behavior becomes a vortex that feeds itself with each confirming thought of powerlessness over a situation. The machine driving this spiral, yes, the mind, is paying attention to that which is out of my control.

As we learn to focus on the breath when we feel overwhelmed, we can begin to place our attention on something other than chaos. We can find something positive to pivot toward. If you are thinking, I do not have anything positive going on right now. My friend, I hear you, but you must understand that this type of thinking is exactly what kept me from moving into a brighter place in my own life. Now is the time to notice all the positives!

My goal during the darkest times in life was to stop the never-ending thoughts of sadness and despair. I would often listen to guided meditations that helped me to feel better in the short term, but then I was back again, alone with my tragic thoughts. A practice that led to longer-lasting peace was breath counting.

The process is simple, as soon as we catch ourselves in a negative mindset, we count the in-breaths (inhalation) and out-breaths (exhalation). We place our attention on the breath, rather than the problems in our life, the to-do-list, what-is-for-dinner, or our-noisy-neighbor. When the mind wanders to our problems, to-do-lists, and neighbors, we bring our attention back to the breath. With practice we can rest our attention on the breath for a few seconds and then for a few minutes. Of course, our mind will wander to all sorts of places, and that is okay. We simply return our attention to the breath and begin counting again. With time we may develop an awareness of the sensations of breathing, such as tingling around the nostrils, coolness of the air entering our lungs, and myriad other sensorial experiences.

As we focus our attention on the breath and sensations of the breath, we begin to balance the nervous system. Wait a minute! Does this mean that the mind and breath are working together? Always! As you begin breath counting try to make each breath slower, deeper, and try to make the out-breath longer than the in-breath.

I like to place one hand on my heart, as a gesture of self-compassion, and the other on my stomach, to feel my belly rise as I inhale and fall as I exhale. This practice is known as belly breathing, it helps engage the diaphragm and creates a natural relaxation response to stress. I have a friend who helps children to manage their anxiety. She will ask the child to place a teddy bear on their belly and then watch the bear rise on the in-breath and then fall on the out-breath. She calls this the teddy bear meditation.

You may be getting the point that our mind and body are constantly feeding each other information and that breath counting not only engages the parasympathetic nervous system to help calm us down, but it also quiets the mind. Yes, my friends, the proverbial two for one deal!

Now you try it. Can you make it through three cycles of in and out-breaths before the next thought arises? Probably not in the beginning, like me, but eventually the practice of breath counting not only calmed my nervous system, it also helped me to slow down the constant chatter in my mind that was running my life. If this chatter had been a real person, I would have sought a restraining order! Even this tiny break from constant negative thinking began to make a difference.

Each day I put a reminder on my calendar to practice breath counting at least three times per day typically during my morning commute, at lunch, and just before bed. As time passed, when I noticed myself getting agitated, I would automatically default to breath counting. Little by little, day by day, I felt more at ease in my skin. After several weeks of this practice, I began to worry less, and this allowed space for new realizations. These realizations became my guidance system and for the first time in life I was empowered with a tool to lower my stress.

MOVE

Humans are built for movement. No matter what our physical ability, there are ways to move the body and feel better. Many of us intuitively jiggle a leg or chew our lips when we are stressed. Why do we do this? Why is movement so important to well-being? Because it dissipates the energy that we so desperately need to shed from our activated nervous systems!

Children are experts at releasing energy by bouncing in their chairs, throwing a toy, or running in circles until they collapse. As adults, many of these activities are considered inappropriate. But there are simple movements that we can utilize to release energy in more appropriate and subtle ways: like slowly tensing and releasing each muscle in our shoulders, torso, buttocks, thighs, calves, and feet. Feel free to take a couple of moments and try this practice right now. Don't forget to breathe!

Oftentimes the first action to restore balance in the nervous system is to change our physical location away from an argument, toxic person, or toxic environment. Perhaps there was a time in life when

PRACTICE PAUSE: MOVE YOUR BODY

I invite you to listen to a piece of music that brings you great joy or think back to a time when you had a favorite song, and you loved to dance to this song! If you are hearing impaired, then I invite you to find a vibration or other sensation that inspires movement. Perhaps the feeling of humming in your own body.

Think back to a time when you had a favorite reason to move your body and you loved the feeling of this movement!

Find a place free from the judgment of yourself or others.

Move your body in whichever way feels most inspiring. It doesn't need to be artistic or even rhythmic. Let the body move in whichever way lightens your heart and brings you joy. Some people prefer to just shake it out.

Start at the top of your head and begin to bounce.

Move to the shoulders and continue the motion down the torso.

Let this movement travel to the other parts of your body. If you are able, shake your shoulders, arms, and hands.

Continue the movement down to the legs and feet.

Shake out whatever you have the ability to shake!

Do this for as long as it feels good and then remember to go back and do it again whenever you feel pent up emotions and energy in the body!

we were physically unable to move away from danger. We may have been at the mercy of another human, place, circumstance, or system of oppression. When we are in a more favorable position, we may find the courage to *move* ourselves to safety. A dear friend once told me, "You are free to change the location of your butt anytime you feel discomfort." I have taken this advice to heart and my personal favorite stress buster is moving myself away from anything and anyone that is disturbing my peace.

Sometimes we have simply forgotten how important motion is to our beingness. When we were children, we were encouraged to get our energy out. When did it become normal to sit still for hours on end, without motion or movement? When did we stop jumping in puddles after a rainstorm? We must remember how to bring this joy of movement back into our lives! We can listen to, or feel the vibrations, of a favorite song and move any part of the body that needs to move whenever we want to move it.

There is yet another aspect of movement that is critical to our healing—change. Once we have an awareness of the state-of-energy we are experiencing, we can begin to choose from a new repertoire of actions to change to a more favorable energy state. If you are feeling lethargic or low energy, invite some movement into your day; go for a walk, shake, or dance. If you are feeling over excited or anxious, invite calming activities into your day, like a bath or a nap. No matter what your energy state is, try to bring some play into your day. Find activities that you enjoy and can work into your daily routine to manage these very real changes in energy.

In my own experience, through the daily practice of working with my breath and moving my body, anxiety began to subside. I began to feel safer in the world and space was created for me to experience more ease. I began to crave movement and change in all parts of my existence. I exercised daily, made plans with friends, and stopped isolating myself from the external world. I tried new things, and in the process, made even more friends with different interests and perspectives on life. I took Djembe (West African drum) lessons just for fun! I reveled in driving my scooter through town, with the wind on my face. Life can be fun-what a concept!

Day by day, a new person emerged. A person that no longer lived in constant fear. A person who was ready to take steps to become liberated from the habit patterns that prohibited a fuller experience of life.

TRUST

Let's revisit the Buddha's Law of Impermanence for a moment. The process of *trusting* that everything changes and that nothing is permanent opens a door to *possibility* for improvement in our own lives. I found it useful to pinpoint exactly what needed to improve in my experience of life, so that I could notice changes whenever they occurred.

After watching my mind and the inner critic's impact on day-to-day reality, I discovered that I carried a sense of heaviness throughout my day, which cast a dark cloud upon all my beliefs, hopes, and dreams. I discovered that when I could notice the heaviness and focus on it, I could trust that there was a different way to live. Neuroscience research suggests that we replace old memories through creating new memories and new experiences. In trusting that there is a new way to experience the world we are clearing the path for these experiences.

It all fits together. We trust that life can be different, and we trust that we can be different. In doing so we open the door to new experiences. New experiences flow to us, and so it is. New memories arrive and the heaviness of the past is replaced with the possibility of the present.

Trust that you have innate wisdom waiting to guide you and the path will reveal itself through this process of reintegration of body, mind, and spirit. This process will take time and effort for both the body and the mind have created adaptations to help you survive in the current environment. Undoing these adaptations will unleash all sorts of thoughts, emotions, sensations, behavioral patterns, and fear responses. However, as you begin to trust in your natural abilities to heal, this belief in healing becomes a thought, a sensation, and a behavior pattern that, in turn, will lessen these outdated responses.

Once I consistently practiced these three actions in daily life, breathing, moving, trusting, a new reality began to emerge. I began to feel sensations of safety in the body and thoughts of comfort and ease in the mind. Thanks to neuroplasticity the more we practice the better it gets! We shift the nervous system from a state of hypervigilance into an experience of calmness.

Our physical environment may not change immediately, but our perceptions will, therefore our experience or interpretation of the world must also change. This is exactly what happened to me! I was now capable of exploring mental and emotional reactions to daily life in a positive space and was determined to continue improving in these areas.

PRACTICE

Listen to the Bodymind. Anthony Thompson Shumate's, "Monumental Moments". Buffalo Bayou Park. Houston, TX.
Photo Credit: R.K. Rodgers

CHAPTER 13

EMBRACING CHANGE

I had sufficient evidence that the combination of nervous system regulation, meditation, and yoga were influencing my experience in profound ways. I could sleep through the night, fits of rage had almost vanished, and for the first time in life I experienced peace of mind on a regular basis. But remember that neuroplasticity takes time. We cannot change a lifetime of thoughts and behavior patterns in a day. Therefore, we must constantly wire new pathways of positive thoughts, speech, and actions to manifest who we hope to become in this lifetime. With this new understanding, I set about crafting an external environment that would support my continued transformation.

I graduated from my doctoral program and faced an uncertain job market and looming student debt. I knew from experience that the stressful pace of a corporate job would put me physiologically back at square one. While I once gauged success by dollars in the bank, I now valued quality of life. As neuroscience predicted, with a balanced nervous system the calmer, rational parts of my brain were back online, and the creative juices began to flow. Ideas for entrepreneurial ventures came to light.

I began to share my experiences with close friends and one suggested that I pitch the idea to teach these techniques at a local college. I went to the program director who believed that these skills would nest well within a course on community engagement. I then set about creating a course to explore the influence of chronic and traumatic stress on our neighbors experiencing housing insecurity and homelessness.

The very same challenges to nervous system regulation that we have explored in this book are magnified when facing the threat and trauma of losing your home. I was thrilled that the university accepted this proposal, and I began teaching in the spring.

The first class was at 6pm at night and my students were a mix of traditional undergraduates and adult learners. During the first session I noticed that one young man was very standoffish. He politely listened to the introductory lecture on the nervous system and the function of the amygdala, yet I noticed that he was looking through me rather than at me. At the break I asked him what type of work that he did, and he explained that he was a facilitator at a middle school for children with behavioral challenges. I asked how he liked working there and he told me that sometimes it was great and sometimes it was heartbreaking, but mostly it was dangerous. He had been kicked, bitten, punched, and at one point received a mild concussion from a chair thrown by one of the students. Talking about the incident brought a change in his demeanor. His jaw tightened, his breathing became quicker, and his eyes began to tear up. He said that he really didn't see how this information about the nervous system could be helpful to these students. I replied that my concern was not for his students but for him.

I then asked if he would be willing to do some belly breaths with me. He agreed. I asked him to place one hand on his heart and the other on his belly, noticing the sensations of the belly expanding as he inhaled and releasing as he exhaled. We then sat slowly inhaling and then exhaling in silence. We must have sat there for a good five minutes, just breathing together. The other students began to return from break and so I took one final breath with him, then smiled, stood up and resumed the lecture.

As the weeks went by this student became more engaged and began sharing details about his own successes with the tools presented in our class. During our final class he shared with me how one of his students was having a meltdown and he then asked the student if he would be willing to do some belly breathing with him. He and his student did the same thing that he and I had done on the first night of class. He shared that he had learned how important it was to work with others from a calm and balanced place, rather than let his nervous system dysregulation escalate the situation. His student had the same experience, he learned how to just sit and breathe until the nervous system returned to balance. This formerly standoffish student hugged me and thanked me for the class.

I walked from the classroom to my car and the air was filled with Night Blooming Jasmine, an indescribably beautiful yet otherworldly scent. If the ambrosia of the gods had a smell, this would be it. A wonderful sensation of warmth radiated from my chest up into my throat and head, and then downward through my torso and lower extremities.

I had helped another human to find a method to reduce suffering for both he and his student. For the first time in my life, I had the experience of meaningful work, not just a paycheck, but a purpose. This is what I had been searching for my entire life, a way to use my talents in service to others.

My teaching schedule was two evenings per week, which offered the flexibility that was critical for my continued self-care activities including meditation, hiking in nature, and further exploration of pathways for spiritual growth. I was in my 50th year of life and felt as if I was just getting the hang of living! I also sensed that I was moving toward even greater lessons and methods to help others. The question was now, how to integrate the Western psychological training of my graduate degree with the Eastern philosophy that had catapulted me into a new reality?

RECOGNITION OF REACTIVE PATTERNS

For starters, we can learn a lot from scholars in the East. In Western psychology, we operate with the flawed premise that humans are either mentally stable or not. If we are not behaving in a way that lands us in jail or a psychiatric facility, society tells us that our mind is in good shape. However, anyone with the power of observation has witnessed the same human in a positive mental state one moment, and completely angry, frustrated, or distraught in the next.

Whereas wisdom traditions such as Buddhism and Yoga view the bodymind as transient and ever changing. Our mental state is the culmination of years of programming and experiences that ebb and flow from day-to-day and moment-to-moment. These wisdom traditions facilitate an awareness that we are not only riding the waves of daily challenges to homeostasis, but we are doing so using the programming from our family of origin, the society that we grew up in, and all our personal experiences gathered along the way. Those of us blessed with human existence have at various times experienced joy and sadness, love and loss, rapture and rage, often within the same 24 hours, as our inner worlds shift to respond to the outer circumstances of our lives.

Another shortcoming in Western psychology is that we spend a great deal of energy analyzing human behavior without regard for the mind body connection that is in large part responsible for creating our individual interpretations of the world.

For example, in the nervous system, if something in the world is deemed urgent, then we tend to that thing first. The Sanskrit word *Vedana* captures the phenomenon of urgency of perceptions, formed as our sense organs come into contact with the outer world. Vedana can be equated to a computer processor that determines how information is prioritized.

Urgent material is processed in the brain in 3/8 of a second and takes half the intensity of a non-urgent experience to get moved to the front of the "pay attention to this first" queue (Libet, 2005). Pleasant material, on the other hand, takes a much slower, half a second to process and must be twice as intense as a negative experience to move to the head of the importance queue. In short, the nervous system prioritizes unpleasant stimuli.

For instance, you may wonder why it is so difficult to move forward after an argument. Why do we continue to ruminate about what was said and who was right or wrong, long after the conversation has ended? Your nervous system will need a stimulus that is twice as intense to replace the importance of the argument, and by the way, each time you think about the argument it refreshes the experience and once again moves it to the front of the queue.

A recent example from my own experience comes from the ever-present fire danger in my little town. I have come to equate the sound of helicopters with wildfire. Every time we have a flareup the helicopters are first on scene to assess the scope of the fire. I can be relaxing at home in the middle of a wonderful conversation and at the first sound of a helicopter that all disappears. I am now fixated on checking my local reporting agencies and electronic apps that track forest fires. Are there times when a helicopter flies overhead that is not associated with fire-fighting? Absolutely, but my brain has deemed helicopters as urgent material and all non-urgent material is pushed aside in an instant, or more accurately 3/8 of a second!

For those of us with nervous systems that tend toward high alert, we interpret most things in our world as urgent, which leaves little space for pleasant experiences, or joy. Let's say that you grew up in a family, neighborhood, or society in which you felt unsafe. This experience had an influence on your developing nervous system, which may have carried into adulthood.

We now understand that our nervous system prioritizes negative events over positive events, and negative stimuli need half the intensity of positive stimuli to make it to the front of the queue. Therefore, your nervous system may consistently interpret the world as a negative place even though there are an equal number of positive events happening at any moment in time. Let that sink in for a moment. In Western psychology we term this automatic priority for negative events a *negativity bias*, which is good for recalling dangerous situations so we can avoid them in the future. In a practical sense, this survival function can also create a life of suffering if we fail to understand how our attention to negative over positive can rob us of the possibility of joy. The question now becomes how to navigate a nervous system geared toward processing danger. We must build awareness of this programming and then take a different action rather than defaulting to programmed behaviors.

SUBCONSCIOUS VALUE JUDGMENTS AS A TOOL FOR BUILDING AWARENESS

It may come as a surprise to you that the nervous system subconsciously assigns value judgments to internal sensations in the body. Biologically we sense positive sensations, like feeling sated after a good meal, negative sensations like hunger while foraging for food, and neutral sensations, which in essence are not deemed important to notice. As a *sentient*, feeling being, we gravitate toward sensations that feel pleasant and avoid sensations that feel unpleasant. With good reason, over time our ancestors who could discern positive from negative sensations had a higher survival rate.

Imagine for a moment that you lacked the ability to notice sensations in the body. Many folks on our planet have this very experience due to neurological disorders or injuries. In such cases it may be difficult to impossible to note what is going on in the internal environment. Sensations are a wonderful biological ability to sense and then adapt to an ever-changing world, but sensations can also be challenging to sit with.

There have been transitions in my own life that bring up the most intense of sensations. Money became pretty tight during my second divorce, after moving from a two paycheck to one paycheck household. During this period, I received word that enrollment was down and my classes would be cut in half. I remember feeling as if I were physically trapped. My arms and legs felt heavy, and it was as if a weight had been placed upon my chest. I still had some money in the bank and a bit of time to find another job, but these sensations of feeling trapped were associated with samskaras and past experiences in the perceptual database. We must begin to ask ourselves if these sensations are accurate appraisals of current events. For this we must explore our conscious value judgments.

CONSCIOUS VALUE JUDGMENTS

We now venture into the world of the human brain with our amazing neocortex that facilitates complex thinking and problem solving. Many of us believe that our thought processes are logic based and unwavering. However, I would like to pose a few questions for you to ponder:

If we each believe that we have good judgment, then why do my value judgments differ from your value judgments? I may believe that a specific political party will be a better choice than you do. Or I might hold a different religious belief.

Are individual value judgments constant? Have you ever received information that caused you to change your mind? What seemed like a good deal one minute is a bad deal the next.

How can we be sure that our value judgments are accurate? Am I being influenced by someone in my family, or a person that I admire to believe something outside of my own habits of thought?

Do we change our minds daily? Have you ever *really* wanted something and then realized that it was the wrong size, wrong color, or simply moved on to something you liked better? Have you been deeply in love with a person one day, and months or years later come to wonder what was I thinking?

In Western psychology we refer to this phenomenon as *cognitive bias* and it might surprise you that researchers have categorized more than 180 different cognitive biases! What can we do with biases/value judgments that may not be stable or enduring? One line of reasoning would be that having awareness of our biases is a good place to start. Why is chocolate cake a great idea one day and an unhealthy choice the next? What sensations and beliefs have changed? In other words, what has changed in our homeostatic world to create this discrepancy?

Our interpretations of the world occur through sensations in the body that are judged by the mind using our cognitive biases to allow for quick processing. Excavating these biases will require effort on our part, and I will speak more on this in a moment. For now, let us utilize the trio of strategies: breathing, moving, and trusting, as methods to provide insight into our biases through the process of introspection.

INTROSPECTION

I mentioned earlier how as a child I went to a Magic 8 Ball to tell me all the answers to the quandaries in my life. These questions evolved as I grew into adulthood, but still I had no clue as to how they could be answered. Should I move to a new state? Change my career? End a relationship? I wanted yes or no answers to these very complex questions. I was going to the wrong source. The truth is that you, just like me, have all the answers within you at this very moment. This moment is the starting point for everything that comes next. Look within to the still voice that exists within every living being. This is where we can find answers and experience a fulfilling life. This is the space between value judgments; our *Inner Space*, where we no longer languish in the question, but instead access a sense of knowing exactly what to do.

ONE GREAT ENERGY AND WE HAVE NO NAME FOR IT

What if we aren't actually all alone during the bad times? What if it isn't up to us as individuals to figure everything out? What if there is a force in nature that can guide us through difficult circumstances if we open our hearts to this possibility? As I reflected upon all the times in life when I felt that there was no way out of a bad situation, I could now see that I was mistaken. In each circumstance a path opened, not to the end goal, but to the next step in the journey. To see this possibility, I had to focus on the path rather than the obstacles. Thanks Chris.

I spoke earlier of yoga as a journey of reconnection with body, mind, and spirit. What if there are indeed answers to our deepest dilemmas? What if we can find a way to reconnect these vital parts of our Being? And what if we, right now in human form, are part of this all-pervasive Intelligence?

For example, my second divorce brought up just about every insecurity that I have cultivated since childhood. How could someone abandon me? Who am I outside of the identity of this relationship? How will I manage financially on my own? Each of these challenges had myriad solutions that became accessible WHEN I quieted the bodymind and connected to the unifying energy of the universe.

When I am really twisted in a knot, I have discovered one common denominator, I am no longer in the present moment. My thoughts are sifting through the past for clues as to what happened or racing into the future wondering what else might possibly go wrong. Whenever this occurs, I must recognize that I have some agency in this situation. I can continue to water the seeds of worry, or I can take contrary action, get back into the present moment, and connect to Infinite Intelligence.

In my experience, quieting the mind is half the battle. Recall that it is darn near impossible to do this when we feel in danger. Therefore, we must first balance our nervous system by doing something to better our situation like resourcing, or breath counting. Whenever I feel sensations of worry, I lengthen the out-breath and begin counting. I notice that my mind is racing and is not helping the situation in the least. I recall that I am not alone. I have access to solutions that are beyond my conscious ability to see from my limited human perspective. I call upon this unifying energy to show me the way. I ask for what I need at that moment, *Help me to trust that there is a way forward and that you will show me the way*. I look at the clock and note that it is 3am and there is not much I can do right now as an action step; so I make another request, *Can you help me to get some sleep, so I can begin to act on this in the morning?* I continue breath counting.

Sure enough, morning comes and again I am faced with a choice to get back into my head or out into the world to not only better my situation, but also to make the world a better place. Since we are integral players in this universal energy then we too have the capacity to influence our environments.

I don't have to look very far for a way to be of service in the world. Every time it snows in my little town, I look for a neighbor who could use a ride to the market or help shoveling their driveway. Ask yourself if there is a family member or coworker who could use a hand? These small gestures not only get us out of self-centered thinking but also mean the world to a friend in need. In doing so, we are not only excavating hidden biases, *I am the only person in the world with problems*, but taking action to create a new reality, after an hour of shoveling snow with neighbors my problems don't seem so extreme.

Through repeated effort, and consistent releasing and relaxing into this space, you will not only come into direct contact with your value judgments, but you will also begin to question what these beliefs mean to you, and what you would like to experience differently. These questions can create fundamental shifts in perception that will transform your life. This, my friends, is how we make the change in our internal environments that can catapult us into a new reality. It is one of our own choosing, rather than defaulting to an outdated program of reactive patterns. We can ditch the Magic 8 Ball because we have all the answers that we seek from this space of integration and connection.

PRACTICE PAUSE: NOTICE WHAT YOU NOTICE

Find a quiet spot and set a timer for five minutes.

Sit in silence and notice the quality of the thoughts that appear in your awareness.

As a thought arises, take a moment to notice the value judgments that you place on each thought. Is there anything in your space that is noisy?

How do you relate to these noises? Are they pleasant, or do you wish they would stop? Or perhaps you really don't mind the noise. Are you hot or cold, or is the temperature just right? What else are you thinking about? Perhaps, something that you wish would happen or perhaps something that you don't want to happen?

Can you come up with a single thought that does not involve a value judgment?

Take a few moments to reflect upon this experience.

Write down anything that you would like to revisit in the future.

What is real and what is an illusion? King's Canyon National Park. Photo Credit: R.K. Rodgers

CHAPTER 14

RELEASING REACTIVE PATTERNS

Cease to stare at one reality to be free to experience something else.

—*Michael A. Singer, founder Temple of the Universe*

We have discussed rumination throughout this book. Rumination is a thought process that the Buddha likened to a second arrow that not only increases suffering after a negative experience but also strengthens that memory through repetition or neuroplasticity. Mike Csikszentmihalyi echoed this sentiment when he suggested that our *conscious attention*, or wherever we focus our mind, determines our quality of life. I found this to be true in my own experiences with rumination. The longer I focused on an unpleasant thought or experience, the more traction it gained in my reality.

For instance, when I speak about my ex-wife during a lunch date with a friend, this topic is consistently on my mind for the remainder of the evening and often into the following day. You can guess how my day went as I continually focused on all the things that "went wrong" during our relationship. I also came to discover that these negative thought spirals disconnected me from the sensations in my body. I was literally in my head without awareness that my body was trying to communicate *Hey, these thoughts are unpleasant, can you please stop it?*

After several months of tracking sensations in the body it became easier to notice when my nervous system had shifted into hyperarousal, for example a clenching of the jaw or tightness in the throat. The hurdle for me was that I didn't become aware of these sensations until *after* a stress response was triggered and I was actively engaged in a negative behavior. In short, there was no space between the trigger and response.

I learned from the abbess at Middleland Chan Monastery that there was a key element required for releasing reactive patterns – the mind. While my awareness of sensations in the body had improved, I had done nothing to address the underlying value judgments about any situation. For example, if I judge my work hours being cut as a negative event, then I miss the opportunity to move into a better job.

Let's recall the negativity bias. To rewire this orientation, we must actively seek out something new, like noticing all the positive, wonderful events happening at this exact moment. Somewhere a child is being born or taking its first steps. A meal is being served to someone who is hungry. Yes, wonderful events are happening all over the world at this very moment in time!

So, what does this all mean? As we begin the work of rewiring, we must catch sensations of nervous system dysregulation *before* it manifests into physical action and question our value judgments about the challenging scenario. This creates a possibility to do something new and expand our repertoire of available responses, which in turn creates opportunities to practice and rewire more appropriate behaviors into the nervous system.

CATCH THE SPARK BEFORE THE EXPLOSION

Is there a way to create space between a trigger and reactive pattern? Fortunately, YES, through the practice of meditation. What are we practicing exactly? In the simplest of terms, we are giving the mind a well-deserved rest. We're quieting down the value judgments, perceptions, worries of the past, concerns about the future, and taking a time out. We are getting calm and practicing stillness, and in doing so, diminishing the metabolic stress pathways in the brain and body. Just talking about a break from all this jumble feels good. It's like we have been running our lives at 110% and then decide to pull the car over to cool the engine.

Here is another point for your consideration. Would it be so bad to rest the mind for a moment? Do we really need to analyze every waking moment of our experience, to infuse the world with our conceptualizations of what is and what will be? What if instead we let our experience be, as it is, without analysis? We might glimpse an expansiveness that is no longer confined by our thoughts, experiences, and judgements.

CATCH YOUR VALUE JUDGEMENTS

There are infinite events happening all around us and within us, at any given time like the temperature in the room, sounds from outside the building, the sensation of our back against the chair, and lots and lots of metabolic processes, such as shifting blood pressure, heart rate, digestion, and oxygen/carbon dioxide exchange. *Subconsciously*, out of our awareness, the nervous system can monitor 11 billion discrete bits of information per second. But our conscious attention can only process 16 bits per second, or about 40 details that happen to float into awareness (Libet, 2005). This is why we rely on a perceptual database, a storehouse of experiences, to compare what we are taking in this moment to what has happened in the past. In short, the limitations of our attention force us to rely on past experiences, to make sense of current circumstances, and you guessed it, this is where value judgments come into play.

In scientific terms, our nervous system transduces physical stimuli in the environment, such as a photon of light that we interpret as vision, into electro-chemical nerve impulses which are then compared by this database as value judgments, such as this is something I like, running our fingers through the hair of a lover, vs. something that I don't like, finding that same hair in a plate of food. Yes, we humans are fickle beasts! How can the same object in our experience turn from lovely to abhorrent?

The abbess once asked me if I could assume an inquisitive mind state about a driver cutting me off in traffic. I once believed that people were maliciously cutting in front of me. From an equanimous mind, it occurred to me that perhaps the driver was rushing to tend to an emergency, or perhaps I was in their blind spot, and they had no idea they had cut me off. Our value judgments are variable and malleable. With this understanding we can begin to view the world as a fluid experience rather than a fixed event. We begin to question our interpretations of the world and with practice can change these interpretations.

MENTAL AND EMOTIONAL SELF-MANAGEMENT IN DAILY PRACTICE

As I reflected upon this decade long journey of self-study, I recalled the original research question, not from my time in graduate school, but the one I had formulated in childhood: Is there a way to be at peace, no matter what circumstances surround us? I am thrilled to share with you that the answer is yes! The tools presented here are by no means the only solution available to live a peaceful existence, but I am a simple person and will put forth the simple path that I now practice in daily life.

HOW TO TWO-STEP

When I was a kid growing up in Texas, the first dance I learned was the two-step. It's a simple yet beautiful method to come into harmony with another human and to glide across the dance floor. In the most basic form, two dancers, locked arm in arm, take two quick steps with the feet, followed by two slower steps, while the body continues to move at a constant speed. When Cowboy Boots meet a slick floor, this dance is a graceful way to skate through a mass of swirling, twirling humans. I now present to you the two-step process that will guide you into harmony with yourself and other human beings so that you too can glide across the dance floor of life.

STEP 1 NERVOUS SYSTEM REGULATION

First and foremost, we must understand the flexibility of our nervous systems and realize that we can exert a direct influence over the emotional reactivity or calmness that we experience on a day-to-day basis. We are that powerful! We can accomplish this through using concrete tools to balance the nervous system, such as breath counting, resourcing, grounding, and tracking, when we are dysregulated.

We must then practice these tools during stressful everyday experiences until they become a habit. Recall how urgent material is processed faster than non-urgent material in the brain? The fast-acting circuits of our emotional brain (limbic system) can and will override the slower, thinking circuits of the brain (neocortex) if an event is overwhelming to our sense of safety. This is an important point and the key to transformation. Trying to think our way out of a stressful or emotional challenge will not work.

What should we do when we are spun into a frenzy or frozen in a state of not knowing what to do? Recognize that this is not the time to act on non-essential tasks. Pause for a moment and give yourself permission to wait. We are not in a place to make rational decisions, so postpone anything that is not a basic survival function until after the nervous system is balanced and we are in a more stable state of mind.

STEP 2 LET IT ALL GO!

At this point in your practice, you will begin to come up against all the old programs, memories of things that hurt you in the past and your reactions to these things, that are stored within the bodymind. Someone may do or say something that brings up an emotion or memory of the past, which until now has been dealt with via old concepts and outdated behaviors. We now have a choice to notice these sensations and emotions as old stuff coming up, or we can choose to stuff them down and continue to respond in the same old way through stored reactive patterns of behavior.

Let's say that you are willing to try this out and choose to experience discomfort as old information coming into your awareness. Good for you! Now what do we do with this experience? Let it go. Feel the feelings, notice the sensations, and understand that this moment in time is a new experience. You are now actively letting go of the past by allowing the body to feel sensations, release old memories, and witness this experience through fresh awareness.

EXERCISE: MAKE A "LET GO" LIST

What are you willing to let go of today? I invite you to:

Take out your journal or a sheet of paper.

List the things that you would like to let go. These can be people, places, things, or constructs of our own minds like past and future. Here is a short list from my own experience: fears, regrets, worries, beliefs about myself, beliefs about others.

Now it's your turn. What are you ready to let go of in service to your own transformation?

Set an intention to actually let go. We can set this intention at any point in the day and especially at the beginning of our meditation practice.

Revisit and expand your list as needed.

My second divorce afforded me a wonderful opportunity to practice letting go of the thoughts, sensations, emotions, and memories of the past. Recall what we just learned about subconscious processing? I was recently walking with a friend and felt sadness out of the blue. I then scanned the environment and noticed a TOMS® Shoes display in the window of a local boutique. I flashed back to my wedding day, when my bride wore TOMS® shoes as we walked down the aisle. In an instant, my stomach twisted into a knot, and I ached for the person that was once my everything. But this is a memory, not reality. I took a deep breath and let the memory go, but I felt the full force of the sensations hitting my heart and then traveling through my body. I continued to breathe until the hard, heavy, feelings in my stomach slowly unraveled into tiny ripples that radiated upward to my heart space and then faded away.

The old me would have stuffed these feelings down and moved straight into distractions. In doing so I would have robbed myself of the wonderful transformation waiting at the end of a valuable release! You now have a new tool in your toolkit- *letting go*. This is your opportunity to breathe, relax, and release outdated information and samskaras to make room for new experiences.

A profound change that I experienced through letting go, was a shift in perception from things-to-do to fun-to-have. Each morning, I make a list of work items, then fill the time in between with fun items, like texting my friend to arrange a movie night next week. Another fun item that I work into my day is parking in the lot farthest from my classroom so I can walk through the flower garden and past the duck pond at the far edge of campus. I make it a point to smell a new flower, from a different bush, each time that I walk through the garden. The world is a buffet of experiences waiting to happen, of which I am an integral part if I make the time for these experiences!

With patience and persistence, this practice has progressed from something that I occasionally remember to do, to something that happens on a moment-by-moment basis. In essence, I have begun to wire hope into my nervous system. I am still not an expert, nor can I say that I have mastered the two-step process, but neuroplasticity is now working in my favor, and my day-to-day reality continues to evolve for the better.

GLIMMERS

Just as we once experienced thoughts and sensations of negative reactive patterns in the bodymind, we may also begin to get glimpses into a new experience, one of excitement, like butterflies in the stomach, or perhaps an inner peace that feels like a lightness in the chest.

Glimmer is a term that has been used to label a micro experience of positivity and well-being in the bodymind (Porges, 2011). We know all about neuroplasticity and we have come to understand the method by which we can actively change our own neural pathways, and practice whatever we want to anchor in. Glimmers are the precursor of these new and positive experiences the bodymind is ready to anchor in. When we get a glimmer, we rejoice and welcome it! Learning is taking place and we are creating a new reality through our bodyminds. This is the time to sit with this new reality, to feel it, notice the sensations, and savor this experience for as long as possible.

Whenever a glimpse of excitement, peace, ease, or any other wonderful sensation comes into my experience I welcome it, and I hold onto it as long as possible. We intuitively know that life is impermanent and that nothing lasts forever, even our own precious human bodies. Fortunately, the same is true for outmoded beliefs and experiences. We thank these defense mechanisms, these outdated reactive patterns, and the people, places, and circumstances that have propelled us toward a new reality.

My Happy Place. Palm Springs, CA. Photo Credit: R.K. Rodgers

CHAPTER 15

ALLOWING A NEW REALITY

The whole of life is but a moment of time. It is our duty, therefore,
to use it, not to misuse it.

—*Plutarch*

CONNECTION IN THE PRESENT MOMENT

The daily practice of nervous system regulation and letting go of all thoughts, beliefs, and practiced notions had begun to yield insight. I observed that the answers I so desperately sought were always available, whenever I could create space for this information to flow to me. An image then hit me, of a pipeline running from my body to a repository of infinite knowledge in the Quantum Field. There was the physical body on one end and the Universe on the other, and the only thing preventing a constant flow of vital information was my chattering mind, a literal shutoff valve in between the two. I then flashed to my first day at the Middleland Chan Monastery, when I asked the abbess what Buddhism was all about, and she replied, "the mind." I sat stunned for a moment. She had explained it so clearly at the time, but I was not yet capable of understanding her answer.

I worked with this visualization for several days and found that during the few precious moments when the stream of thoughts ceased to flow, yogas chitta vritti nirodha, serenity was present and a knowing emerged that all was well. Everything was exactly as it should be, and that more would be revealed if I could maintain this connection. This was a turning point in my practice. I now understood the importance of staying connected to this pipeline of well-being, and the only way to do so was to remain in the present moment.

Mindfulness is the practice of witnessing the present moment, while dropping all preconceived notions and judgments about the experience. This sounds so simple, but we must also consider how emotions influence our ability to be mindful.

Shakyamuni Buddha likened the mind to a bowl of water and emotions as perturbations that disturb clarity. When water is still the reflection in the water is a true representation of the surrounding world. This metaphor beautifully explains our perceptions of reality and *mind states*. When the mind is angry it is as though the water in the bowl is boiling and we can no longer see the reflection of the outer world. When the mind is passionate it is as if the water were dyed a bright color, and we no longer see reality, but a distorted version of the world.

The point is not to eradicate emotions. Emotions are a vital part of our survival and make us completely unpredictable and fascinating. The point is to understand how emotions can influence our thoughts and behaviors and to use this information to our advantage.

ESCAPING THE WHIRLPOOL

While difficulties in life are very real, suffering arises through the forces of emotion and the vehicle of the mind. Recall the Buddha's explanation of the second arrow? Without this awareness of what is driving our states of discontent, we are doomed to endlessly loop scenarios recounting what happened, prophesizing what will happen next, and catastrophizing how bad it will continue to be. Each cycle leads to intensified emotions and a tightening spiral of catastrophic thinking.

Recall that the mind and body are a continuous feedback loop of homeostatic information. Through simple observation I can notice when I am breathing shallowly or holding my breath, which are direct indicators of a shift in states of body and mind. Whenever I catch myself holding a breath, I try to catch the thought, sensation, or notice what external scenario is happening. I can then take a few belly breaths, redirect my thinking to the positive, and recover quickly.

But what about those times that we don't catch dysregulation quickly? How do we get out of this whirlpool of suffering? We can go to the root of the challenge and cease the stream of thoughts, yogas chitta vritti nirodha. But for those of us who are not yet Zen masters, we need some tips and tricks to interrupt the cycle; lines to pull us out of the whirlpool.

TIPS AND TRICKS

LABELING

There are myriad processes to find our way back to safety. Let us begin with the experience of sensations. We have learned how to track the sensations in our body and now have practiced to the degree that we can notice when different sensations arise. An unpleasant sensation is a sure sign that we are delving into uncomfortable material in the bodymind. One process that works well for me is *labeling*. I notice a negative sensation or my body tensing up and quickly examine the thought at hand, typically something out of my control. I label this mind state *Fear* or *Worry*. It is not reality, for at this moment I am safe. I am worrying about some future event that has not yet happened, and will not happen if I can take calm, purposeful action. I take a few belly breaths, steady my mind, release the thought, and let the sensation release itself.

In my experience it is not so much a sensation, but the thoughts that accompany sensations that are gasoline on the proverbial fire. The sooner we label a negative mind state and release the thoughts and emotions associated with that mind state, the sooner we can return to balance.

Over time this practice becomes less painful and more therapeutic, much like exercising an injury to build strength. A sensation will arise and for an instant there will be a hint of anger, irritation, sadness, or fear but a quick release facilitates a return to baseline peace, and a balanced nervous system. The more that we practice this method, the easier it becomes to move through mental and emotional disturbances. As we repeat this process, we develop an ability to get comfortable with the process. We relax and release with greater confidence and ease.

EMOTIONS AS VISITORS

Another helpful trick is to envision emotions as visitors. Each of us possesses a complex subconscious world of sensations and emotions that will routinely percolate to the surface. While these experiences may feel infinite, the good news is that few of us are stuck in perpetual states of happiness or sadness. Emotions are visitors that we can choose to invite into our experience or to leave our experience. The game is to catch the unwanted visitor before they settle in. Is there a foolproof way to accomplish this? Practice! The sooner we catch a negative emotion beginning to bubble up and replace it with something positive, the less likely we are to spiral into suffering.

DAMN, I'M LUCKY!

On occasions when I fail to catch a negative thought or sensation and I'm heading toward the whirlpool, I say a mantra, prayer, or affirmation repeatedly to overpower the negativity. Our brains can only focus on one thing at a time, so if we are earnest in keeping the positive in the forefront of the mind this will shift our thinking on the spot. One of my favorite mantra or affirmations is *Damn, I'm lucky*. Looping this thought in my mind affirms that somehow, some way, things always tend to work out for me. It's true! I have been in some seemingly unsolvable situations that I miraculously made it through. Perhaps even more amazing is that when I look back on these catastrophes they no longer seem like a big deal.

A good friend uses the affirmation, "I Am Divinely Guided and Divinely Protected." She says that this keeps her connected to a Power that is watching over her always. While thoughts are nice, beliefs are powerful! The trick of this process is that the mantra or affirmation should be something that you believe in your heart. When you are repeating the mantra notice what sensations arise in the body. If you have chosen a meaningful mantra, there will be an immediate release from the tension and frustration of a negative thought. The mind is that powerful!

WRITE IT OUT

Journaling or getting your thoughts and emotions down on paper has been shown in empirical studies to increase optimism and feelings of well-being, and to lower stress and feelings of helplessness (Den and Lengelle, 2023). There is no special instruction other than to write from the heart and try not to edit your feelings; let them flow out of your heart and onto the page.

I once was going through a particularly challenging break up and spilled my emotions so strongly onto the page that the pen tore through to the next sheet of paper. But, damn, I felt better after putting these feelings down on paper! This writing session preceded the actual breakup by 15 months. When I went back and read the feelings that I was experiencing, I could not believe that I chose to prolong the relationship.

Perhaps there is subconscious wisdom in the words that we express through journaling. I now make it a point to go back and read my journals on a regular basis to not only note progress, but to keep an eye out for blind spots in my cognitive justification that allow me to override critical information coming through the pen.

LESS THINKING, MORE EXPERIENCING

The ultimate Zen trick is to create a routine to remain in the present moment, each and every moment of the day. This whole experience is based upon the principle that the present moment is not a thought, but rather an observation. Right now, I am sitting in my living room, writing a book, and enjoying a hot cup of tea. The past is not in my living room, nor is the future.

You may be wondering how I can write a book without going into the past or future. Let's revisit the concept of the pipeline between a still mind and the Infinite. When replaying the past in my mind, I am pushing words around on a page. With a clear mind, I have a portal to unlimited inspiration and the words flow onto the page. How do we know which mode we are in? The difference between outmoded thoughts and inspiration are discernable through the quality of the thoughts and sensations in the body. Replaying old tapes feels crummy in the bodymind. Clearing the mind and allowing new ideas to emerge feels great!

EXTERNAL STIMULI VS. INTERNAL SERENITY

As we put these principles into practice, we have two final hurdles to address. First off, many of us need external stimuli to feel happy, like the presence of another person, or an exciting event like being on vacation. In the absence of something happening, we become uneasy waiting for something external to give us that burst of *dopamine*, experienced as giddiness or joy. If we want peace, no matter what, then we must learn how to be happy just sitting in a chair without any external stimuli. That's the epitome of serenity.

Second, many of us don't truly understand the purpose of the conscious mind. Contrary to what we've been taught, the mind's job is not to analyze everything. Its job is to clearly see whatever it is focused upon, much like a scuba mask.[2] When we put on a scuba mask and place our head underwater the mask helps us to see whatever swims in front of the mask. The mask doesn't attempt to see or to know every single object in the ocean. Similarly, our mind is a tool to observe whatever is happening right now in our field of experience, rather than to analyze or predict everything that can possibly happen in the future.

This brings us back to the simplicity and utility of the present moment. As a hard-core thinker, I have found that after hours of mulling over ideas, feeling the sensations that arise, and theorizing about exactly what all this means, I physically and mentally wear myself out, and find myself right back where I started, in the here and right now. An intelligent person might wonder, why not just go straight to the present moment, rather than run yourself ragged? And they would be correct. The present moment is the only place where we can experience peace and serenity.

---

2. Analogy courtesy of Darryl Anka

MENTAL AND EMOTIONAL SELF-MANAGEMENT PRACTICE (MESM)

Let us now view these tips and tricks as a continuation of our mental and emotional self-management practice. First, we balance the nervous system. Second, we build the capacity to steady our mind. Third, we actively watch emotions and develop skills to release those that are not in accordance with peace and ease. And finally, we let go and rest in the present moment. During my time at the monastery, I received an easy mindfulness process to follow—notice thoughts arising, counter negative thoughts with positive, rest in the positive. This combination of Eastern philosophy meets Western trauma-informed practice, has saved my life.

I must constantly pay attention to the thoughts and sensations that are part of everyday experiences, notice the negative and accentuate the positive. For instance, I received an email from a colleague asking for help with a project outside the scope of my job. I stopped to notice my reaction. My face became flushed, my temper flared, and my mind flashed to a dozen past experiences when I have been overworked and asked to put time into someone else's project, putting me further behind on my own work. I must pause and realize what is happening at this moment. I understand that remaining in a frustrated mind state is not only bad for my health, but isn't helping the situation at hand. I take a few belly breaths and then begin resourcing. I think about my little dog's face, the warmth of her body sitting next to me, and her unconditional love for me. In an instant the bodymind shifts from agitation to love. I am now in a mind state that can ask clarifying questions, determine if I can manage the extra task, and perhaps not only help another, but gain some benefit from the transaction as well. I can also decide if this request is beyond my comfort level and then politely decline this request. Clarity leads to simplicity in thoughts and actions.

EXERCISE: MENTAL AND EMOTIONAL SELF-MANAGEMENT MEDITATION (MESM)

In this exercise we will use meditation to release stress and stored patterns from the body and mind.

Set a timer for 16 minutes.

Use the first minute to settle into your body, noticing any places where you are holding tension and give yourself permission to breathe into these areas to let the tension dissipate.

Breathe.

Notice the breath without trying to manipulate or modify. Let it gently flow into and out of the body, like waves from the ocean.

Relax the body and mind.

Allow yourself to become the observer of all thoughts and sensations that arise. When a thought arises, notice the thought, but don't give it any juice to develop into a storyline or movie that you play in the theatre of your mind. You are the observer of the thought that is no more than that—a thought.

When a sensation in the body arises, notice the sensation, but don't give it any juice to develop into a storyline.

When a sense of ease arises in the bodymind, relax, and give yourself permission to savor this experience. Don't cling to the experience.

When a sense of discomfort arises in the bodymind, relax and remember that you are the observer. Don't cling to the experience for it will be replaced by another.

> When a distressing thought or sensation arises, know that you are safe and know that with time this experience will pass.
>
> These patterns are based upon outdated information and patterns of survival. We know that neuroplasticity is a real physiological process, and that we have the ability to rewire our nervous system by continuously shifting our thought processes from distressing to safe.
>
> Breathe in and know that you are loved.
>
> Breathe out and know that you are safe.

ACCENTUATE THE POSITIVE

Finally, I recommend that we constantly practice reorienting our mind toward positive experiences. We must become adept at noting what a positive experience feels like and where we feel it in the body. Spoiler alert, when you become good at resting in the positive, you are on the precipice of an ability to shift your emotional state at will!

The trick is to notice when the body tells us that something is amiss and immediately do something about it. Some folks call this being in tune with our gut. The ultimate goal is to catch an unpleasant sensation quickly and redirect the bodymind to a pleasant state. How the heck do we do this? The first step is to stay out of the past or the future, and second to remain grounded in the present moment!

The abbess at the monastery would often say, "Keep your mind wherever your butt is." As we progress in this practice, we begin to spend more time enjoying wherever our butt is.

It should make a great deal of sense that whenever we are present with an experience, we have more time to experience whatever is actually happening outside of the perceptual database of the past. Buddhists call this practice "just tree." Rather than noticing what type of tree it is, whether you like or dislike this type of tree, or whether you once fell out of a tree just like this one, we experience just looking at the tree. In doing so, we may notice more qualities about the tree, like the smell of resin, or the texture of the bark, or we might notice a small bird tucked in the branches. We miss these aspects of reality when we are busy creating our version of the tree based upon past experiences in the perceptual database.

On the sign: I am beautiful. But I will hurt you. (please be careful around cacti)

If only people came with warnings! Photo Credit: R. K. Rodgers

CHAPTER 16

MORE WILL BE REVEALED

In the early days of mental and emotional self-management practice I was happy if I didn't have a childish meltdown when someone happened to block the aisle at the grocery store. With further practice I could notice when my mind was racing, and I could identify the accompanying sensations in my body. The ability to identify this mechanism of suffering helped to slow the chatter and differentiate thoughts and emotions, as well as track which preceded which. I came to discover that a thought could trigger an emotion and a sensation in my body could not only trigger a thought, but also an emotion, and a behavior. I was unraveling the chain of events that led to the habitual patterns that had previously existed outside of conscious awareness.

Many of these *memory capsules* of thought, sensation, and emotion are stored from a past traumatic experience, perhaps as far back as childhood. There have been events in my life that have triggered a reaction like *disassociation*, a daydream-like state, or a *freeze* response, when I have literally been unable to move.

For example, an argument with a romantic partner could propel me into a freeze state, subconsciously recalling how past quarrels had led to abandonment and physical harm. Today, I know that these are not reality, but rather artifacts from experiences in childhood.

During one impactful Somatic Experiencing (SE) session, my therapist and I discovered a memory capsule from late childhood. My little brother, who was a toddler, had disappeared from the house. My mother came running to me frantically screaming that he was missing, and we had to find him. We set about searching the house, front and back yards, but there was no sign of my brother. My mother then turned and screamed in my face that this was all my fault and if anything happened to him that she would never forgive me.

Thankfully, my brother had wandered to the next-door neighbor's house and was found moments later enjoying cookies in the kitchen. However, the gravity of being held personally responsible for my brother's disappearance made a lasting impression on my nervous system. You may be thinking, well, of course, this wasn't your fault. But at a formative age, I fully believed that not only was it my fault, but I should have known better. I should have maintained constant vigilance rather than playing outside with friends.

My therapist suggested that this event became a blueprint for adult life, informing relationships, jobs, and environments that I was drawn toward. It is a rare and wonderful experience to witness the subconscious database from a conscious place. This information became invaluable in processing negative talk, sensations of doom, and narratives of never enough that had been operating in my subconscious for decades.

As this memory capsule revealed itself during therapy, an intense tightness rose from my chest and neck into my head. A searing hot pain radiated upward like someone had shoved their hands inside my skull and tore apart the tissue in my brain. This event had been buried in my body for years waiting to come up at a time when I could safely process the experience. Now was the time and in the safety of my therapist's care I could feel the intense sensations and let them flow through me and out of me.

You may wonder if you too have experiences in your bodymind waiting for a safe time and place to emerge for processing. Recall the steps that you can take each day: move your body, take some belly breaths, and trust that as you open your heart more information will arise.

SUBCONSCIOUS MATERIAL

Neuroscientist Lisa Feldman Barrett's book, *How Emotions are Made: The Secret Life of the Brain* (2018), explains in beautiful detail how sensations in the body, coupled with our past experiences drive the predictions that our brain makes about any situation. This book helped me to understand a biological model of the brain as a predictor of possible outcomes, using the perceptual database as a repository that informs our actions.

Furthermore, Dr. Barrett adds an important dimension to understand the physiology of the brain-body connection with regards to trauma, "the brain keeps the score, and the body is the scorecard" (Barret, 2023). I must add a wrinkle to this *mind-body dualism*, or scientific separation of the mind and body that continues to plague neuroscience. As someone with preverbal trauma, my nervous system acts in ways that my conscious mind cannot apprehend. I can be hit with an experience of dread with such intensity that it will awaken me from a deep sleep. I have no recollection of a bad dream or anything in my external environment to cause me to worry, but sensations in my inner arms, inner thighs, neck and chest are that of skin crawling terror.

An impactful author on the topic of emotions and trauma is Pete Walker. His book, *Complex PTSD: From Surviving to Thriving* (2013), terms these experiences *emotional flashbacks*, a literal reliving of experiences from the past in the present moment. Post Traumatic Stress Disorder (PTSD), as we have come to understand it, can result from one overwhelming experience to the nervous system. A flashback from PTSD will typically involve mentally, physically, and emotionally returning to re-experience this one event.

Complex PTSD (C-PTSD) differs in that there are multiple traumas that the bodymind has experienced, many of which may be stored at a subconscious level. Emotional flashbacks are a sudden and often prolonged return to those frightening experiences from childhood that do not include a visualization or memory, thus making it difficult to realize that we are re-experiencing an event from the past. In essence, we believe that we are actually there, in the past, although physically we are in a completely different place and time.

The emotional flashbacks that I experience often present an overwhelming sense of sadness or dread, seemingly out of the blue. I can be sitting on the porch, enjoying the birds and in an instant feel that something is dangerously wrong. Without an awareness of the cause of this feeling of danger, it can conjure up a cascade of physiological and mental gymnastics. My heart begins to pound, and my mind begins to catastrophize about anything and everything out of my control. *What if I can't pay my bills over the summer? What if this book is never finished? What if Democracy fails in the United States?*

After becoming familiar with the concept of the emotional flash-back, I discovered that these would occur in my experience multiple times per day. For example, a recent realization of a recurring emotional flashback centers around preparing and eating food. In child-hood, dinner time was an opportunity for my dysfunctional family to gather. My mother and stepfather barely spoke to each other, but when they did it was argumentative and demeaning. I tried to disappear by saying as little as possible, but invariably, I would be dragged into the smear campaign and chastised for my own shortcomings, such as what I was wearing, my hair style, or the way that I ate. Occasionally the conversation would escalate into a shouting match, ending with broken plates and glasses.

Later in life I had a relationship with a partner who was critical of the way that I prepared food and the types of food that I prepared. She was also prone to starting arguments at the dinner table. But it didn't end there. Choosing a restaurant for an evening out was a battle, as well. I would make a suggestion, she would offer another suggestion, I would then go along with her suggestion, and she would snap back with some-thing along the lines of, "Why am I always the one that has to make a decision about where we eat?" Not surprising, I developed digestive issues during this relationship, and a tendency to disassociate during mealtimes. With this awareness, I can see how experiences from both childhood and adulthood have created anxiety around mealtimes and my relationship with food.

Through practice I am now aware when emotional flashbacks both in life and regarding food occur. I understand this experience of a flash-back for what it is, a record of the past, and I make a point to replace this old experience with something beautiful. For example, regarding food, I didn't do anything drastic like remodel the kitchen or take a cooking class. I simply noticed the sensations coming up, understood where this emotional response was coming from, and gave thanks for the peace in my life and for the wonderful food that was awaiting me on the table.

EXERCISE: FLASHBACK MANAGEMENT IN THE
TREATMENT OF COMPLEX PTSD
(COURTESY OF PETE WALKER, MA, MFT).

Say to yourself "I am having a flashback."

Remind yourself, "I feel afraid, but I am not in danger! I am safe now here in the present."

Own your right/ need to have boundaries.

Speak reassuringly to the Inner Child.

Deconstruct eternity thinking.

Remind yourself that you are in an adult body and ease back into your adult body.

Gently ask your body to: Relax, Breathe, Slow down, Find a safe space.

Feel the fear in your body without reacting to it.

Resist the Inner Critic's drasticizing and catastrophizing.

Use thought stopping.

Use thought substitution.

Allow yourself to grieve.

Cultivate safe relationships and seek support.

Learn to identify the types of triggers that lead to flashbacks.

Figure out what you are flashing back to.

Be patient with a slow recovery process.

I am now rewriting the story of mealtimes with each loving meal that I prepare and enjoy.

If you believe that emotional flashbacks may be part of your own experience, I invite you to explore Pete Walker's work on C-PTSD, and his practice for addressing emotional flashbacks.

At this point in the book, you may be wondering where the line is between chronic stress, that is so prevalent in society, and *traumatic stress*, which is based on one or more experiences that overwhelm the nervous system. How do we know if we have experienced trauma in childhood or if our adult experiences could be labeled a traumatic event?

I recommend that we view our lives as a journey of experiencing and learning from these experiences. This is enough to facilitate the journey. I moved through the world seeking answers to these questions long before I was given a clinical diagnosis and will continue to learn, grow, and heal for as long as I have the willingness to do so.

We, as a society, must also begin to honor those who have experienced trauma. Each of us must adopt a trauma-informed lens when dealing with others. While someone who does not have trauma may be able to cognitively teach their "butterflies to fly in formation", as prescribed by Dr. Lisa Feldman-Barrett, this is an impossibility for someone who's nervous system is running as fast as possible to avoid butterflies.

Bessel van der Kolk's book, *The Body Keeps the Score: Brain, Mind, and Body in the Healing of Trauma* (2015), has a good bead on this aspect of traumatic expression in the body. Much of the childhood trauma that I experienced happened before my brain could form memories. Although my brain was at one point in time the genesis of the tensing of muscles and steady stream of catastrophizing thoughts; my body has now given me insight into these subconscious responses to threat. The body IS the gateway to these experiences, and the method by which I can process threatening sensations and release them in a safe way.

Whether we conceptualize the body as the scorekeeper or scorecard, the conscious brain of a traumatized person may be cloaking subconscious memories of what happened in the past. In my experience, the body tells the tales that the brain cannot or will not disclose.

POST TRAUMATIC GROWTH

I am happy to share that I have experienced great success in understanding the psychobiology of my own Post Traumatic Stress (PTS). I have learned to recognize and interrupt emotional flashbacks, and to process and release these stored experiences. Through mindful awareness of the sensations that arise, I can catch an emotional flashback, take steps to disidentify with the flashback, interrupt the pattern of getting sucked into the mental and emotional turmoil, and then process the experience as a flashback rather than reality. I am thrilled to report that both the frequency and intensity of emotional flashbacks have diminished dramatically through this practice.

I have also experienced the fruits of rewiring the nervous system by choosing positive over negative in the environment, my thoughts, my beliefs, and my actions. I avoid toxic stimuli such as news media, shock entertainment, people, places, and circumstances that activate my nervous system. I no longer tolerate toxic jobs, destructive relationships, nor catastrophizing and negativity from my Inner Critic.

As my *zone of resilience*, or operating range of a balanced nervous system, has continued to expand, I spend more time in a state of calm and ease. When unexpected events do happen, I have greater capacity to deal with these inevitable ups and downs of life. The little girl that walked on eggshells all her life is now growing into a serene adult who is no longer preoccupied with potential dangers. She can relax into the present moment.

With persistent practice I became capable of interrupting distressing patterns of alternating sensation, emotion, and thought. I could sense that my perceptions of each of these were faulty and that if I could interrupt a pattern, I could change the meaning of the pattern and choose a different outcome.

Going back to the concept of emotional flashbacks, whenever I experience a feeling of uneasiness, I know that this is not me. I know it is an artifact of a long past experience. With this awareness, I can shift my attention to something positive, like the warmth of my bed, or the beautiful day awaiting me tomorrow. When I am awakened in the night by a sensation or dream, rather than panic, I now label it as old information. I thank these sensations for coming forward and letting me know of their presence. I shift my attention to gratitude for the experience, knowing that each release is a step toward healing. I say to myself, "You are releasing and healing and can go back to sleep. All is well."

I was gaining control of my mental and emotional world. As I began to interrupt previously subconscious activities, I now had a choice in how to behave. My perceptions were becoming clearer. I could notice a negative sensation and ask, *What do I need right now? A drink of water, a nap, a meal?* I could also notice negative seeds in the mind, like, *This is the slowest checkout line in the world* and choose a more positive thought like, *Thank goodness that I have money to buy groceries.* As the survival brain became less activated, my logical brain was more accessible, and I was now able to engage consciously with my thoughts.

We are now ready for the deeper work yet to come! As we evolve mentally and emotionally, realizations will begin to arise. Like layers of the onion, we will continually uncover truths about our unique journeys, the pain and joy of past experiences, and the limitless potential in the present.

We must gently, but bravely lean into these experiences. We must find the edge where we can tolerate discomfort, experience it with curiosity, and allow it to shape us into something new. This process is the same for a muscle, a thought, a behavior, or any event that we experience in our bodymind. Relief from the suffering in our lives comes from developing greater flexibility in body and mind.

It is now time to expand our attention beyond the bodymind, to explore the importance of networks and to recognize that life is not something to conquer in isolation. Let us now move our attention to the support systems that will assist us in achieving harmony in our inner and outer worlds.

CHAPTER 17

YOUR NETWORK TO ACHIEVE
WELL–BEING

W e have spent several chapters discussing the mind-body connection and how unconscious survival patterns can influence our entire existence. We have also learned specific tools to create change in our internal worlds. We are now ready to tap into resources in the external world, which will not only facilitate personal growth, but create connection to the abundance that surrounds us.

COMMUNITY

Community can take many forms. Sometimes it is a group of friends that not only fills our cup when we are together but also forms a circle around us in times of need. It can be a faith-based family, a school-based group of parents and teachers as well as extended caregivers, a local fellowship, or an online group of support and encouragement. The Buddhist *Sangha*, fellow travelers on the path to liberation, are one such example of community. I am privileged to be an active member of multiple community groups and sangha around the world.

For a moment, let's bring our attention back to the nervous system and the importance of connection. Stephen Porges, PhD explains through Polyvagal Theory, how our connection to other humans is the neurological basis for physiological balance and well-being.

High Sierra Trail, Kern River Valley, CA. Photo Credit: "Selfie Stick" Alidad Nories

His theory is based upon the function of the Vagus Nerve, the main parasympathetic nerve in the body, that regulates heart rate, breathing, digestion, and immune function. The Vagus Nerve originates in the brainstem and connects to every major system in the body including the throat, heart, lungs, liver, stomach, spleen, kidney, and small intestines. This nerve is, therefore, the conduit for information traveling from the subconscious, survival portion of the brain, the *brainstem*, to every other major system in the body. As previously mentioned, the *parasympathetic* response calms us down. For example, the Vagus Nerve directly influences the cardiac pacemaker. It literally slows the heartbeat and creates a feedback loop of calm to the rest of the body.

We have discussed dysregulation of the nervous system in simple terms such as activation of either the fight or flight or freeze response. Dr. Porges adds a critical social dimension to this model. He notes that we operate within a social engagement system, where our interactions with others can influence our interpretation of the outer world. For instance, if someone pushes you aside, then smiles, noting that you were about to step into traffic, the nervous system response is very different than when someone pushes you aside and then scowls at you. In essence, our bodies take cues from other human beings and then shift states according to our perceptions of their actions and facial expressions of harmony or aggression.

In Polyvagal Theory, co-regulation, or the tendency to attune to another's nervous system, is vital for our own sense of safety. The key word for co-regulation is *safety*. As expected, proximity to unsafe people can trigger a stress response. However, the opposite occurs in the presence of safe humans, we experience a relaxation response in our own nervous systems. This enables us to better manage stress and our emotional responses during challenging situations.

Dr. Porges explains how for those of us who have experienced traumatic events, our nervous system may be prone to misread the external world. We have adapted to an unsafe world with a tendency to misinterpret neutral and positive experiences as unsafe. From the Polyvagal perspective our past experiences literally change our perceptions of safety around other humans. Knowing this, we can begin to question our own interpretation of what is safe and what is not safe. As with value judgements, we must again question our interpretation of any situation. Are we accurately reading the room or bringing forth old programming into new relationships?

Let's talk a bit about isolation. Humans are social animals. We travel in packs and rely upon one another not only for our daily existence, but also for a sense of safety. When we experience disconnection from other humans whether it be through environmental challenges, pandemics, stress, or any form of self-isolation, our nervous system interprets this absence of human connection as dangerous. Conversely, when we connect to safe humans the restoration of this connection helps us to feel happier. Finally, we can use this information to decide how we will choose to be in the world, as an isolated person, or as a human surrounded by safety and community.

As mentioned earlier, I teach a college course in community service where students study the scholarship of helping others and then practice these principles through giving service in a caring and collaborative way. Students choose a local non-profit in their own communities as opportunities to share their talents with the organization. Some students donate expertise, such as legal aid or tax help, others contribute manual labor, such as building houses or working in communal gardens, and all are encouraged to engage face-to-face and heart-to-heart with those receiving helping services.

Students are asked to reflect upon their evolution in experiences and attitudes throughout the course, and one of the biggest surprises that students report is the sense of elation they experience when being of service to others. The literature refers to this phenomenon as the *helper's high*, or a direct experience of well-being while giving service to others (Dossey, 2018).

Oftentimes, students will begin the course feeling that they don't have time for actively engaging in community service, and that they would much rather just drop off some clothes or canned goods for course credit. However, after interacting with their neighbors, both giving and receiving support, these students report feeling a part of, and integral to the health of their communities. This supports the idea that we are social creatures and feel at our best when helping others. I would like to share with you one student's reflection on her experiences while giving community service,

People need to feel empowered, in truth, I needed to feel empowered. Looking at a specific issue like food accessibility and seeing how two couples connected with others in their church to create a network of support and resources to establish the Food for Life Ministry food pantry was encouraging. These were just "regular folks" who saw a need and tapped others on the shoulder to see what they could offer to help address the problem. To see how successful they have been and the attitudes of the people in that organization, I was humbled and empowered. That sounds paradoxical but true. I was humbled by the willingness and energy that these senior citizens exhibited that was so unselfish, where I had seen myself as selfish. They made efforts and were bold to make changes, where I felt unable to really be effective. Witnessing their efforts, I became empowered. The positive energy that comes from loving others and loving yourself is powerful.

This is a life-changing course if you allow it to be. Because of this experience, I will continue to participate at the pantry. It is helping me personally and with my work life, too. I look at what I can do well and offer my talents, and I will encourage others in their strengths. Life can be good. It is possible with little action steps that are leaps of the heart!

During this course, I encourage students to bring their family and friends along to share the experience of giving service to others. Not surprisingly, this shared time has brought parents closer to their children, improved relationships with coworkers, and created a sense of social responsibility and pride for being civically engaged in their own communities.

This brings to light the notion that community can be found in myriad places. Note how *support* is the common theme here. Not only will you give support to others, but you will receive support in return. Your

Teaching the MESM skills to families
Photo Credit: community service student.

community should be a source of hope. Often this support is not available in our biological family, close friends or romantic relationships, therefore, we must venture into our communities to discover sources of unconditional love and understanding. In my experience, opportunities for this type of support have expanded as I have grown in the capacity to offer love, hope, and understanding to others.

TEACHERS

There are community support groups, family members, loved ones, faith-based organizations, spiritual teachers, healthcare providers, complementary and alternative healthcare practitioners, and a multitude of mind-body workers who can assist us in our journey to well-being. In my experience, these humans are an integral part in the process of uncovering and healing hidden wounds.

Beloved teachers, Guishan Island, Taiwan
Photo Credit: R.K. Rodgers

Some of you may wonder if we can do this work alone. A great deal of the work must be done through our own efforts, the most obvious example being our own commitment to self-directed neuroplasticity. Personal growth is first and foremost an inside job. But it is important to learn from others as well. Safe and nurturing human connection is part of our healing process.

I have been supported through myriad school, work, and family connections, and been blessed with mentors in my college career such as Dr. L.W. Gertmenian, who not only taught the basics of economics, but wove a moral story of obligation to serve others into every lecture that he taught. Mike Csikszentmihalyi and his belief in the potential for goodness and well-being in mankind was remarkable, given that he was shot in the leg as he narrowly escaped Nazi invaders in his homeland. And then there is the abbess at Middleland Monastery who is always so patient in her explanations, and so diligent in translating Buddha Dharma for we Westerners. Mentors and teachers abound in our social circles. It is up to us to find venues to connect with each of these opportunities. A monastery, church, community organization, or work group can all serve in this capacity.

Mt. Baden-Powell 2023 Blizzard, Angeles National Forest, CA. Photo credit: R. K. Rodgers

NATURE

We need to wake up and fall in love with the earth. Our personal and collective happiness and survival depends on it.

—*Thích Nhất Hạnh*

Another critical part of my healing is the time I dedicate to getting into nature. And yes, nature is also a great teacher. When we commune with our natural environment, we begin to sense that we are *a part of* rather than *apart from* our planet. In my experience, this interaction with our own wildness or animal nature is much like a drug—once you take it you immediately feel better.

Three years ago, I made the decision to move to a little mountain town in California. This gives me the opportunity to hike two to three times per week in the summertime and then do the same but on snowshoes in the wintertime. One of my favorite spots on the mountain overlooks the Los Angeles basin on one side and the Mojave Desert on the other. I had no idea how this experience would change me but suffice it to say that my trips down the mountain make me long for the clean air and pine trees that are now part of my everyday life.

I acknowledge the challenges we have in modern society, and our urban lifestyle can create barriers to being in nature. However, I challenge you to find a patch of grass, or a tree, whether it is a backyard or a local park. Go and spend as much time as you can because nature provides a reset. We spend so much time in our heads that we forget that we are this living breathing being that is a part of something much bigger than ourselves. Nature provides a beautiful reminder of this and in doing so helps to restore our own natural balance.

I have also discovered while in nature that it is easy to feel a connection to a presence greater than myself. I feel a wisdom in the trees that tower over me that have witnessed hundreds of years of floods, fires, and the occasional hiker passing below. I understand that I occupy a fleeting moment on the planet, and a sense overcomes me that all is well in the universe, all is being taken care of, and that my own life is part of this natural ebb and flow of energy.

I go to nature as frequently as possible and when I am out of touch with nature for a couple of weeks, my emotional balance is the first thing to go. I get agitated more readily, and I start losing touch with the big picture. I am just another living organism on this magnificent planet we call Earth, and I can be a benefit to this planet, and be of service to all my fellow sentient beings. I choose to be a good steward of our environment because it is our breath of life. No trees, no breath. No green space, no breath. So, we *are* nature and getting into nature reminds us of who we are.

PRACTITIONERS

In my twenties I experienced debilitating migraine events. The pain was so intense that I would lie in a ball, huddled in a dark room for three days until the pain would subside. I had no idea what was triggering these events or how to get past them. One day I walked into a store that had chair massagers and sat for 10 minutes as the wheels rolled over the excruciating bumps on my back, shoulders, thighs, and calves. My body was in agony and within an hour I was laid up with another migraine event. I came to learn that the rollers had pushed into my lymph system releasing toxins that had built up for years. Once I was past this migraine event, I felt an amazing release of tension and illness, and a noticeable reduction in the frequency of migraine headaches. I continued to go for the occasional massage and discovered that with each uncomfortable experience, my recovery was quicker, and the migraines were fewer and farther between. This was enough to get me hooked on massage.

At this point in my life, I had no idea that trauma could be stored in the body, or I would have jumped into bodywork immediately. After I became aware of the multitude of bodyworkers and healers available, I made it a point to find those that are geared toward releasing trauma from the body, thereby restoring balance to the energy systems.

Over the years I have utilized many types of body work. The concept of inner life energy, such as *prana*, *shakti*, or *chi*, is foreign to many in the West, but these ancient medical and wisdom traditions embrace this energy as a critical source of well-being.

You can learn more about energy work through Ayurvedic medicine, Yoga philosophy, or the rich history of energy practices such as *Qigong* and *Tai Chi*. For the purposes of this chapter, we will focus on energy work specific to the release of trauma stored in the bodymind.

Again, as with any new direction in healing, it is important to find a teacher or practitioner that works with your values. I have occasionally come upon a practitioner that did not seem like a good fit for whatever reason. The important premise with any new healing experience is to keep trying, both with new modalities and practitioners.

It is equally important to explore how you are feeling about trying something different. If there is resistance, then honor that. If you are willing but are having a hard time connecting with a practitioner, then honor that. I have learned that pushing myself into situations rarely re-sults in a positive outcome. With this in mind, I have compiled a list of practices that have yielded positive changes within my own bodymind:

Acupuncture
Acupressure
Craniosacral release

Chiropractic care (mental, emotional, structural support)
Flashback Management for Complex PTSD (Pete Walker)
Myofascial massage
Integral bodywork
Light therapy/ Binaural sound therapy
Mantra
Mudra
Osteopathic manipulation
Qigong
Somatic Experiencing (Dr. Peter Levine)
Structural Integration (Ida Rolf)
Tai Chi
Talk Therapy
Tension, Stress, and Trauma Release (Dr. David Berceli)
Trauma Resiliency Model ® (Elaine Miller-Karas)
Vipassana Retreat
Yoga asana

If you are looking for something fairly easy to get into that yields immediate benefits, I recommend Tai Chi. I took my first Tai Chi class in Santa Monica, California at a community center. The class was paced very slowly, the moves were rhythmic, and it was fun to move in unison with the instructor and my fellow students. After a few minutes of these movements, I felt an amazing sense of relaxation and calmness in body and mind. I recall thinking that any activity that moves this slowly and was this much fun couldn't possibly yield lasting results. I walked to my car at the end of the class and felt a little stoned. I actually remember contemplating whether or not it was safe to drive home in this condition!

Another wonderful practice that costs nothing and yields great benefits is the technique of *mantra*, speaking a word or phrase that transforms our bodymind state. It is beautiful to understand the words that you are speaking, but feeling the vibration of your voice in the cavity of your body yields wonderful results. One of my favorite mantra is, *Om*, the cosmic sound of the universe. In Buddhism the three syllables A, U, Ma, represent our body, speech, and mind. Each time we chant, Om, we can think of enlightened beings and aspire to transform our own body, speech, and mind to that of an enlightened being. Chanting is also a way to harmonize our energy with others, and therefore, Om is often chanted in sets of three in the beginning of a spiritual gathering.

The list of techniques and practitioners above is certainly not exhaustive. I continue to discover new methods that I wish to explore each year. I do not wish to urge you into a specific direction but rather, I ask that you keep an open mind. Opportunities will arise to practice specific methods whenever you become ready.

Fear not, volumes of books on these topics are available if you wish to do some research before you begin your journey. Similarly, the practitioner or teacher that you choose will differ from my own practitioner. Each of us are so different, there is little point in urging you to try one modality over another.

Throughout our journeys, it is important to realize that information about injurious past experiences is remembered by the nervous system and centered in places we may not be consciously aware of. Therefore, energy work can range from mild to intense and the experience can dislodge deeply buried survival responses, sensations, and stories. Likewise, you may just have a lovely experience without much fanfare.

When you are ready to dig deeper, then deeper work will become available to you. When we are ready and willing, the teacher will appear. What

---

PRACTICE PAUSE: CHANTING OM

Center your mind.

Take a deep breath.

Sing the mantra "Om (oh-m) slowly allowing the vibration to permeate your body as you exhale.

Repeat the mantra three times.

The vibration of the mantra coupled with deep breathing makes this a wonderful calming and centering technique.

I can share with you is that this type of work has helped me to excavate those areas of stored aches and pains in the body that were tied to injuries of the past. I have discovered that humans are like onions, with stored patterns and beliefs, and that each layer uncovers deeper and deeper levels of stored energy that are no longer serving us. The body work that I have experienced over the years has helped me to lighten the load of the past and grow into more positive experiences of health and well-being.

You now have an overview of the myriad paths available to begin to restore your own well-being. I have experimented with many practices, courses of study, therapies, retreats, medical and spiritual communities, and through trial and error, have come up with a routine that keeps me on the path of well-being:

> Sleep.
> Hydrate.
> Address the excessive human stress response using MESM tools.
> Meditate daily (15 minutes minimum) AND whenever the body or mind becomes agitated.
> Connect to the One Great Energy.
> Yoga asana 2-3 times per week, AND whenever the body or mind become agitated.
> Reflect daily to note what is working, what is not, and connect the dots on triggers, patterns, and practices that change the day for the better.
> Use my toolbox for negative thoughts and when agitated say a mantra, prayer, meditation or write a gratitude list or a journal entry.
> Take a walk, get in nature, and read inspirational books.

YOUR TURN

What does a day in the life of optimal self-care look like for you? Now is the time for you to progress on your own healing journey. The therapies and adjunctive treatments outlined in this book overlap in many ways, and no one program is recommended over another. I have also detailed how the wisdom traditions of the world have led to profound changes in my well-being, and these too are complementary lesson plans for living.

Each chapter in this journey has led to a new realization and continued path of healing.

Through this work, I have allowed grace to enter my life through connection to a power greater than myself. This Power is loving, caring, nurturing, and flows through all sentient beings and natural resources on this planet. Through this connection I have healed relationships with all who have harmed me and asked forgiveness from all that I have harmed.

What's the point of this journey that I have shared with you? Each of us must find the most appropriate way to influence our own nervous systems. Now that we understand that we have the power to re-shape the pathways of our brain and nervous system, we get to choose which path we are on, fear or love. We get to be who we want to be in the world!

Bridge Fire, 2024 Photo credit: R.K. Rodgers

CHAPTER 18

THE BREAKTHROUGH

What I am telling you is that you have a choice. Once you master this process it will have a profound impact on your life.

—R.K. Rodgers

It was a normal day working from home. I held a class on Zoom and graded a few assignments. A friend texted to see how the fires were impacting our town and mentioned that I had a place to stay if needed. I thanked her and assured her that all was well. I then had a teleconference with my therapist. During our session I noted that the sky had suddenly turned blood red outside of my office window. We continued our conversation and wrapped up around 4:00pm. The room had become unusually dark, like 9pm dark rather than 4pm dark. I turned on a few lights and made my way to the front porch. I stepped outside and the smell of soot hit me. I then saw that it was raining, not water drops, but big clumps of ash and debris. The forest fire that had been a safe distance away this morning now seemed ominously close. But there had been no mentions of danger on the Watch Duty app that I had been tracking periodically throughout the day.

I went back into the house and checked the local blog. Other towns-folk were getting worried as well and several recommended gathering important items like birth certificates, passports, medication, and pet food just in case the evacuation notice came through.

I continued grading assignments and made a mental list of what I would put together if the call to evacuate did happen. I thought to myself, we typically get a watch first, then a warning, and then the evacuation order. *I have plenty of time.* That's when the jarring tri-tone sound blasted from my phone. It was 4:44pm and the message was level three: evacuate immediately.

I stared at the phone for a good minute, making sure that I wasn't misreading the situation. No, the wording was very precise. It was time to pack up and leave. For a moment I thought about hooking the little travel trailer to my truck but immediately decided that it was time to get focused and follow orders. I packed the essential paperwork, an overnight bag of clothes, toiletries, dog food, and the dog, and was out the door within 10 minutes.

A flurry of calls and texts came through as I packed, "Did you get the evacuation notice? How soon are you leaving? Do you need anything?" It is amazing how many neighbors in the midst of their own evacuations had stopped to check on me. That's the beauty of this little town. I checked on my neighbors to the east and west of my place, and they too were packing up or had already left town. I jumped into the truck and began to head down the hill to my friend's house who had called hours earlier.

The procession of vehicles inching out of town was met by a steady stream of fire trucks speeding in the opposite direction, toward the fire raging on the west end of town. At this moment I felt at peace. I had a plan, a place to go, and the knowledge that everything possible was being done to save our town.

That night I made a mental review of the day and was surprised by how smoothly it went. The typical trauma responses: pounding heart, dry mouth, confusion, second guessing, double checking, worrying, indecision about where to go, what to take, and what to leave behind, were all absent. Something had shifted in me. I was calm, collected, and responded in the most appropriate way for this circumstance.

The next morning, I awoke and for a brief moment went into worry mode, *what if the house is gone?* In that instant I said aloud, *"NO! We're not going there!"* Instead, I shifted my attention to gratitude for the safe place where I spent the night, for all of the firefighters that were still out there on the mountain battling this fire, and for another day to get up, get a cup of coffee, and do something positive with my life, like check on my neighbors and teach a full day of classes on Zoom!

The blaze raged for several days, but the firefighters and emergency management crews fought a heroic battle, and we were able to return to a town with relatively little damage. For the first time in a long time life felt manageable. I had no control over the forest fire, but complete control over the way that I acted during this experience.

Most of my life had been spent mercilessly trapped in a catastrophic thought cycle, a trauma response to a long-ago event. My teacher, Geshe Dorji Damdul, once commented that we are bullied by our minds. I cannot give you the exact date or time that I shut down the bullying, but the change has been remarkable. I now have agency to choose my thoughts and to redirect thinking that is not beneficial to well-being. I have been liberated from the bully that ran my life for so long and am free to live in peace.

My wish is that this story inspires you to begin your own healing journey and to share your unique gifts with the world. I hope that you will commit to working with your mind, to make it a calm, peaceful, environment. I implore you to find the bravery to work with your body, to listen to it, and to let it guide you to become an integrated being. May you develop the ability to choose what kind of day you will have, rather than be at the mercy of conditioned thoughts and habit patterns.

I wish you a hearty laugh on a daily basis. I also wish you profound peace, happiness, and joy. I hope that you will join me in the aspiration that all beings be freed from suffering, that all beings be truly peaceful, and all beings find true, lasting happiness. Sarva Mangalam!

RESOURCES AND
FURTHER READING

Barrett, D. (2010). *Supernormal stimuli: How primal urges overran their evolutionary purpose*. WW Norton & Company.

Barrett, L. F. (2017). *How emotions are made: The secret life of the brain*. Houghton Mifflin Harcourt.

Barrett, L. F. (2023). The Neuroscience of Trauma, Big Think Interview. https://bigthink.com/the-well/neuroscience-of-trauma/

Bowes, P. (2015). The Man Who Leads with No Limbs. Retrieved from: https://www.bbc.com/worklife/article/20150318-leading -without-limbs

Brewer, J. A., Worhunsky, P. D., Gray, J. R., Tang, Y. Y., Weber, J., & Kober, H. (2011). Meditation experience is associated with differences in default mode network activity and connectivity. *Proceedings of the National Academy of Sciences, 108*, 20254-20259.

Britton, W.B., Lindahl, J.R., Cooper, D.J., Canby, N., Palitsky, R. (2021). Defining and measuring meditation-related adverse effects in mindfulness-based interventions. *Clinical Psychological Science*. https://doi.org/10.1177/2167702621996340

Bryant-Davis, T. (2020). The Treating Trauma Master Series. National Institute for the Clinical Application of Behavioral Medicine. Retrieved from https://www.nicabm.com/program/treating-trauma master/?network=o&utm_source=bing&utm_medium=cpc&utm_ campaign=316289981&ad_group_id=1350200529996674&utm_term =nicabm&utm_content=&del=bing316289981

Canady, V. A. (2019). APA annual stress survey finds 2020 election one major cause. *Mental Health Weekly, 29*(43), 6-7.

Chödrön, P. (2000). *When things fall apart: Heart advice for difficult times.* Shambhala Publications.

Chödrön, P. (2007). *The places that scare you: A guide to fearlessness in difficult times.* Shambhala Publications.

Cohen, R. A. (2014). *Subcortical and limbic attentional influences, the neuropsychology of attention.* New York, NY: Springer.

Csikszentmihalyi, M. (1990). *Flow: The psychology of optimal experience* (Vol. 1990). New York: Harper & Row.

Damdul, D. (2019). Nalanda Diploma Course. Tibet House India.

Den Elzen, K. & Lengelle, R. Eds (2023). *Writing for Wellbeing: Theory, Research, and Practice* 1st Edition.

Routledge. Dossay, L. (2018). *The Helper's High.* Elsevier Explore. Volume 14, Issue 6. November 2018. Pages 393-399.

Easwaran, E. (2007). *The Bhagavad Gita:(Classics of Indian Spirituality)* (Vol. 1). Nilgiri Press.

Everly, G. S., & Lating, J. M. (2013). *A clinical guide to the treatment of the human stress response* (3rd ed). New York: Springer.

Farb, N., Daubenmier, J., Price, C. J., Gard, T., Kerr, C., Dunn, B. D., Klein, A. C., Paulus, M. P., & Mehling, W. E. (2015). Interoception, contemplative practice, and health. *Frontiers in Psychology, 6*, 763.

Farias, Miguel, David Brazier, and Mansur Lalljee, 'Introduction: Understanding and Studying Meditation', in Miguel Farias, David Brazier, and Mansur Lalljee (eds), *The Oxford Handbook of Meditation*, Oxford Library of Psychology (2021; online edn, Oxford Academic, 14 Mar. 2019), https://doi.org/10.1093/oxfordhb/9780198808640.013.1, accessed 15 July 2020.

Felitti, et al. "The Adverse Childhood Experiences Survey", 22 Oct. 2019, https://www.rockefellerfoundation.org/wp-content/uploads/2021/03/ACE-Questionnaire.pdf

American Psychological Association. "Stress in America 2020: A National Mental Health Crisis", 1 Feb. 2021, https://www.apa.org/news/press/releases/stress/2020/report-october.

Felitti, V. J., Anda, R. F., Nordenberg, D., Williamson, D. F., Spitz, A. M., Edwards, V., & Marks, J. S. (1998).

Relationship of childhood abuse and household dysfunction to many of the leading causes of death in adults: The Adverse Childhood Experiences (ACE) Study. *American journal of preventive medicine*, 14(4), 245-258.

Gazzaley, A., & Rosen, L. D. (2016). *The distracted mind: Ancient brains in a high-tech world*. MIT Press.

Gazzaniga, M. S. (2000). Cerebral specialization and interhemispheric communication: does the corpus callosum enable the human condition? *Brain*, 123(7), 1293-1326.

Gendlin, E. (2007). *Focusing*. New York: Bantam Books

Haines, A. (2009). Asset-based community development. *An introduction to community development*, 38, 48.

Hallowell, E. M. (2005). Overloaded circuits. *Harvard business review*, 11, 1-10.

Harris, N. B. (2018). *The Deepest Well: Healing the long-term effects of childhood adversity*. New York: Houghton-Mifflin Harcourt.

Hawkins, J.A. (2021). The Discovery and Implications of Neuroplasticity. In: Brain Plasticity and Learning. Palgrave Macmillan, Cham. https://doi.org/10.1007/978-3-030-83530-9_1

Hesse, H. (1951). *Siddhartha*. New York: New Directions.

Hölzel, B. K., Carmody, J., Evans, K. C., Hoge, E. A., Dusek, J. A., Morgan, L., & Lazar, S. W. (2010). Stress reduction correlates with structural changes in the amygdala. *Social cognitive and affective neuroscience*, 5(1), 11-17.

iChill App is a free resource available for Android and Apple devices https://www.traumaresourceinstitute.com/ichill-app/ichill-app-1

Iyengar, B. K. S. (2002). *Light on the Yoga Sutras of Patanjali*. London: Thorsons Publishing Group.

Iyengar, B. K. S. (2005). *Light on life: The yoga journey to wholeness, inner peace, and ultimate freedom*. Rodale.

Kabat-Zinn, J. (2000). Indra's net at work: The mainstreaming of Dharma practice in society. In G. Watson,

S. Batchelor, & G. Claxton (Eds.), *The psychology of awakening: Buddhism, science, and our day-to-day lives* (pp. 225–249).

Kabat-Zinn, J. (2009). *Wherever you go, there you are: Mindfulness meditation in everyday life*. Hachette Books.

Kalia, M. (2002). Assessing the economic impact of stress-The modern-day hidden epidemic. *Metabolism-Clinical and Experimental, 51*(6), 49-53.

Kajimura, Shogo & Masuda, Naoki & Lau, Johnny King L & Murayama, Kou. (2020). Focused attention meditation changes the boundary and configuration of functional networks in the brain. Scientific Reports. 10.10.1038/s41598-020-75396-9.

Lama, D., Tutu, D., & Abrams, D. C. (2016). *The book of joy: Lasting happiness in a changing world*. Penguin.

Lazar, S. W., Kerr, C. E., Wasserman, R. H., Gray, J. R., Greve, D. N., Treadway, M. T., . . . & Rauch, S. L. (2005). Meditation experience is associated with increased cortical thickness. *Neuroreport, 16*(17), 1893-1897.

Lebit, B. (2005). *Mind Time: The Temporal Factor in Consciousness (Perspectives in Cognitive Neuroscience)*. Harvard University Press.

LeDoux, J. E. (1994). The amygdala: Contributions to fear and stress. *Seminars in Neuroscience, 6*, 231-237. http://dx.doi.org/10.1006/smns.1994.1030

Levine, P. A. (2010). *In an unspoken voice: How the body releases trauma and restores goodness*. North Atlantic Books.

Levine, P. A., & Frederick, A. (1997). *Waking the tiger: Healing trauma: The innate capacity to transform overwhelming experiences*. North Atlantic Books.

Manoogian, J. III, & Benson, B. (2016). Cognitive Biases Codex. Retrieved October 22, 2018. Chromeextension://efaidnbmnnnibpca jpcglclefindmkaj/https://www.sog.unc.edu/sites/www.sog.unc.edu/files/course_materials/Cognitive%20Biases%20Codex.pdf

Mark, G. (2015). Multitasking in the digital age. *Synthesis Lectures on Human-Centered Informatics, 8*(3), 1-113.

McEwen, B. S., & Stellar, E. (1993). Stress and the individual: Mechanisms leading to disease. *Archives of internal medicine, 153*(18), 2093-2101.

Middlebrooks, J. S., & Audage, N. C. (2008). The Effects of Childhood Stress on Health Across the Lifespan. Project Report. *National*

Center for Injury Prevention and Control of the Centers for Disease Control and Prevention.

Miller-Karas, E. (2015). *Building resilience to trauma: The trauma and community resiliency models.* Routledge.

Miller-Karas, E., & Leitch, L. (2009). A case for using biologically based mental health intervention in post-earthquake China: evaluation of training in the trauma resiliency model. *International journal of emergency mental health, 11*(4).

Miller-Karas, E. (2023). *Body Literacy Helps to Regulate Emotions.* Psychology Today. Online. December 24, 2023 https://www.psychologytoday.com/us/blog/building-resiliency-to-trauma/202312/body-literacy-helps-to-regulate-emotions

Miller-Karas, E. (2023). *Mindfulness Through a Trauma Informed lens: Trauma survivors benefit from a trauma-informed perspective.* Psychology Today. Online. December 26, 2023. https://www.psychologytoday.com/us/blog/building-resiliency-to-trauma/202312/mindfulness-through-a-trauma-informed-lens

Moseley, G.L., Butler, D.S. (2015). Fifteen years of explaining pain: the past, present, and future. *The Journal of Pain, 16*(9), 807-813.

Ogden, P., Minton, K., & Pain, C. (2006). *Trauma and the body: A sensorimotor approach to psychotherapy (Norton series on interpersonal neurobiology).* WW Norton & Company.

Ogden, P. (2020). The Treating Trauma Master Series. National Institute for the Clinical Application of Behavioral Medicine. Retrieved from https://www.nicabm.com/program/treating-trauma-master/?network=o&utm_source=bing&utm_medium=cpc&utm_campaign=316289981&ad_group_id=1350200529996674&utm_term=nicabm&utm_content=&del=bing316289981

Patanjali, Translated by Charles Johnston (2022). *The Yoga Sutras of Patanjali.* Compass Circle.

Payne, P., Levine, P. A., & Crane-Godreau, M. A. (2015). Somatic experiencing: using interoception and proprioception as core elements of trauma therapy. *Frontiers in psychology, 6,* 93.

Poole Heller, D. (2019) *The Power of Attachment: How to Create Deep and Lasting Intimate Relationships*

Porges, S. W. (2011). *The polyvagal theory: neurophysiological foundations of emotions, attachment, communication, and self-regulation* (Norton Series on Interpersonal Neurobiology). WW Norton & Company.

Porges, S. W. (2004). Neuroception: A subconscious system for detecting threats and safety. *Zero to Three, 24*, 19-24.

Qin, P., & Northoff, G. (2011). How is our self-related to midline regions and the default-mode network? *Neuroimage, 57*(3), 1221–1233.

Rodgers, R. K. (2019). *Mental and Emotional Self-Management: An Examination of Psychological and Physiological Outcomes*. The Claremont Graduate University ProQuest Dissertation Publishing. 10843838

Rodgers, R. K., & Kettering, V. L. (2017). Mindfulness training gets an upgrade: Innovations in mental and emotional self-management (MESM) to combat stress in organizations. *Journal of Strategic Innovation and Sustainability, 12*(2), 97-114.

Rodgers, R. K., & Kettering, V. L. (2019). *Mental and emotional self-management (MESM) illustrated manual*. Los Angeles: Way of Well-Being.

Rodgers, R. K., Kettering, V. L., & Hunter, J. P. (2016). Pioneers of Contemplative Practice in Business: A Phenomenological Study. *MindRxiv Papers*. https://doi.org/10.31231/osf.io/dbqp3

Ryff, C. D., & Keyes, C. L. M. (1995). The structure of psychological well-being revisited. *Journal of personality and social psychology, 69*(4), 719.

Sadhguru. *What is Hatha Yoga*. Retrieved from https://isha.sadhguru .org/in/en/yoga-meditation/yoga-program-for-beginners/hatha-yoga

Sapolsky, R. M. (2004). *Why Zebras Don't Get Ulcers: The Acclaimed Guide to Stress, Stress-Related Diseases, and Coping*. Holt paperbacks.

Scaer, R. (2005). *The trauma spectrum: Hidden wounds and human resiliency*. W. W. Norton & Co

Shatz, Carla (2017) *Pathways from the eye to the brain*. https://stanmed .stanford.edu/carla-shatz-vision-brain/

Shonkoff et. Al. (2014) https://46y5eh11fhgw3ve3ytpwxt9r-wpengine
.netdna-ssl.com/wp-content/uploads/2005/05/Stress_Disrupts
_Architecture_Developing_Brain-1.pdf

Shonkoff, J.P. (2011). Protecting brains, not simply stimulating minds. *Science, 333*(6045), 982-983.

Siegel, D. J. (2010). *The Mindful Therapist: A Clinician's Guide to Mindsight and Neural Integration (Norton Series on Interpersonal Neurobiology)*. WW Norton & Company.

Spinazzola, J., Van der Kolk, B., & Ford, J. D. (2018). When nowhere is safe: Interpersonal trauma and attachment adversity as antecedents of posttraumatic stress disorder and developmental trauma disorder. *Journal of traumatic stress, 31*(5), 631-642.

Tandon, S. (2013). Personal Interview *Basic concepts of yoga*. Riverside, CA. University of California Riverside

Trauma Resource Institute (TRI) in Claremont, CA. https://www
.traumaresourceinstitute.com/crm/

Trungpa, C. (2007). Shambhala: The Sacred Path of the Warrior. Mass Market Paperback.

Turel, O., Brevers, D., & Bechara, A. (2018). Time distortion when users at-risk for social media addiction engage in non-social media tasks. *Journal of psychiatric research, 97*, 84-88.

van der Kolk, B. A. (2015). *The body keeps the score: Brain, mind, and body in the healing of trauma*. Penguin Books

van der Kolk, B. A., Stone, L., West, J., Rhodes, A., Emerson, D., Suvak, M., & Spinazzola, J. (2014). Yoga as an adjunctive treatment for posttraumatic stress disorder: a randomized controlled trial. *The Journal of clinical psychiatry, 75*(6), e559–e565. https://doi.org
/10.4088/JCP.13m08561.

Walker, P. (2013) *Complex PTSD: From Surviving to Thriving: A Guide and Map for Recovering from Childhood Trauma*.

Wallace, B. A. (2005). *Genuine happiness: Meditation as the path to fulfillment*. John Wiley & Sons.

Wallace, B. A. (2006). *The attention revolution: Unlocking the power of the focused mind*. Simon and Schuster.

Wallace, B. A. (2016). A Brief Exploration of Shamatha, Episode 41. Retrieved October 22, 2018, from https://media.sbinstitute.com /courses/spring2016/41/

Wallace, B. A. (2022). *The art of transforming the mind: A meditator's guide to the Tibetan practice of Lojong.* Shambhala.

Watts, A. W. (2019). 2.3.5 Zen Bones. Retrieved from https://www .alanwatts.org/2-3-5-zen-bones/